CREATIVE MINISTRY

Creative Ministry

HENRI J. M. NOUWEN

DOUBLEDAY & COMPANY, INC., GARDEN CITY, NEW YORK

Jesus said to Simon Petrus:

When you were young
you put on your own belt
and walked where you liked;
but when you grow old
you will stretch your hands
and somebody else will put a belt round you
and take you where you would rather not go.

(*John* 21:18)

To Seward, Helen, and Anne Hiltner
in memory of
James Seward Hiltner

ACKNOWLEDGMENTS

This book would never have been started without the stimulation of the summer school students of the University of
Notre Dame, who by their enthusiasm encouraged me to
write and keep writing during six hot weeks, and who convinced me that spirituality can be discussed with a sense
of humor. This book would never have been finished, however, without the honest and straightforward criticism of the
Chicago priests, which made me rethink different issues and
rewrite different chapters.

I owe much to the members of the Moreau Community for
their hospitality, expressed not only by offering a quiet room
in which to write but also by supportive friendship when
writing did not seem very easy. I am especially thankful to
Louis Putz for making me feel at home, to Jim Buckley for
his constant help, and to Bob Antonelli for his personal
interest, which made me beat the deadlines.

I also want to express my deep appreciation to Charles
Sheedy and Jim Burtchaell for their invitation to give the
lectures, to Jack Egan and Don NcNeill for their valuable
suggestion for corrections, and to Betty Bartelme for her skillful help during the final stages of the manuscript.

I am very thankful to Rita Gorkowski and Carolyn Dals-
gaard, who spent many hours typing and retyping the man-

uscript, and to Jeff Sobosan, who was so generous as to interrupt his own writing to reshape quite a few of my crooked sentences.

The Frank J. Lewis Foundation, sponsor of the pastoral theology program at the University of Notre Dame, offered the financial support for the preparation of this text.

I have dedicated this book to Seward Hiltner, teacher and friend, who introduced me into the field of pastoral theology; to his wife Helen and daughter Anne, who taught me much through their friendship and trust; and to his son James Seward, who made me realize that the length of life is less important than the intensity and sincerity with which it is lived.

TABLE OF CONTENTS

CONTENTS

INTRODUCTION

The main concern of this book is the relationship between professionalism and spirituality in the ministry. Since many very concrete experiences and events made my interest in this relationship grow, I would like to start with one of the cases that will illustrate the theme that runs through the following chapters.

One day during the past year a parish priest presented to a small group of pastors, of which I was a member, a report of his hospital visit to a twenty-six-year-old married woman who suffered from the fatal Hodgkins disease. The priest, a very intelligent pastor, was quite aware of the fact that this young woman would never leave the hospital and that she probably would die within the coming year. He brought the report of his pastoral visit to the group because he wanted to consult his fellow ministers about how to be of real help to his parishioner in the months ahead.

He described the young woman as a very happy, open person with a good sense of humor and full of energy. He wrote down parts of his conversation with her, word for word as far as he could remember, and concluded with the honest confession that he had felt extremely nervous during the visit and very uneasy and dissatisfied as he had left her alone in the ward.

When we studied this pastoral visit more closely the conversation between the priest and his sick parishioner gave the impression of a long and painful attempt to avoid the reality that a very attractive young woman was soon going to die. They talked about the nurses, the food, the pains, the possibility of getting some sleep, and a great deal about how things would be later when she would be home again. It was obvious that the pastor himself was hardly aware of his avoiding the real issue; but in reading his own report over and over again, he discovered what really had taken place, and during the discussion with his colleagues it was possible for him to become aware that he probably could have been of more help to this woman if he had known a little more about pastoral care for a dying patient.

But then, somewhat surprisingly, one of the group members asked the priest, "Say—I wonder if you are really aware of the fact that *you* are going to die, too, perhaps not within a year but in any case pretty soon." Suddenly, all the discussions about skillful pastoral care stopped and there was a long silence. Then the priest said: "Perhaps not—perhaps I am more afraid to talk about death than my parishioner is, and perhaps I do not want her to remind me of my own mortality . . ."

This response gave a dramatic shift to our "professional" discussion and made us more and more aware of the fact that he who wants to be a real minister to a dying patient can never be so when he has not been able to face his own death and relate in a Christian way to this undeniable reality. And it did not take long to realize that the question about ministry was intimately related to the question about the spiritual life of the minister himself.

This is only one of the many examples that have made me ask if spiritual guidance and professional formation in the ministry are not so closely related that any separation will, in the long run, do harm to both aspects of the daily life of the man or woman who wants to be of Christian service to his fellow man.

Perhaps we have to say that one of the main reasons for the many frustrations, pains, and disappointments in the life of numerous Christian ministers is rooted in the still-growing separation between professionalism and spirituality. However, this separation is quite understandable if we look at the development of theological education during the last decade.

First of all, many seminaries have given up the routine of the spiritual exercises that structured the daily life of the student who wanted to prepare himself for the ministry. Daily hours of meditation, the recitations of long prayers, and regular services were often forced upon students as an essential condition for the saintly life at which they were asked to aim. Often it was suggested that only through this prayer-life could a man protect himself from the many dangers of the great world, and that no minister would succeed in the long run if he were not faithful to what generations of ministers had found to be a support in their busy lives. But, when times changed and the life of the minister developed in new ways, it became less and less obvious how the many hours of piety were related to the daily concerns of the parish life. Ministers began to feel that prayer was more and more experienced as an escape into the safety of the interior life and a way of avoiding the burning issues that should stir the Christian conscience and be a challenge to engage in creative action. They would say: "Let us not close our eyes in order to indulge in nice and gratifying thoughts about God and his mysteries, but let us keep them open to the growing needs of the world around us. Why spend our time in rather dull and fruitless hours of meditation and contemplation when we could use our time better to train ourselves in the necessary skills and techniques that help us to be of real service to our fellow man?" It is no wonder that chapels became less popular places to visit and spiritual directors had fewer clients, and that, instead, much more attention was paid to supervized pastoral training in hospitals, prisons, parishes, and special city projects.

But there is another story, too, usually told by those ministers who for many years have been deeply immersed in the activities, worries, and concerns of the daily life of their congregations or neighborhoods. The multiformity of their work, the different forms of activities they became involved in, the great variety of persons they met, and the broad range of problems they touched finally made them wonder how they could live a unified life under such conditions and how their own most personal integrity could be maintained in the middle of so many contrasting stimuli. Many of these men have given so much of themselves in their daily, often very demanding, pastoral activities that they feel empty, exhausted, tired, and quite often disappointed. This fatigue strikes so hard because thanks are rarely expressed, progress is seldom obvious, and results not often visible. Even when one knows how to be a good counselor and how to respond meaningfully to the needs of individuals and groups, even when one is fully prepared to be an agent of social change, the most burning question remains: "What moves me to do all this; where do I find the strength to find unity in all my diverse activities; how can I find the strength that helps me to be a man like Paul, who, in the middle of all his adventures, kept himself one through his unshakable faith in Christ and Him crucified?"

Going back to regular prayers? Spending more time with the reading of the Scriptures? More meditation and hours of silence? Days of recollection? Retreats? Many have tried it but felt lost. It seemed as if they were saying: "If I cannot find God in the middle of my work—where my concerns and worries, pains, and joys are—it does not make sense to try to find Him in the hours set free at the periphery of my life. If my spiritual life cannot grow and deepen in the midst of my ministry, how will it ever grow on the edges?"

The question that seems to come up more and more in the circles of those who want to dedicate their lives to the Christian ministry is the one that lies beyond professionalism. There is hardly a doubt any longer that being a minister calls for careful preparation, not only in terms of the knowledge and understanding of God's word but also in terms of the ministerial relationships through which God's word comes to man. Just as a doctor, a psychologist, a psychiatrist, and a social worker need special skills to be of real help to their fellow men, so a priest or minister will never be able to fulfill his task in a responsible way without the necessary training in the core functions of his ministry, such as preaching, teaching, caring, organizing, and celebrating. Pastoral training centers have provided many priests and ministers with the necessary professional preparation and offered them many ways to make their work more satisfying, meaningful, and effective.

But although the main concern of ministers over the last years has been to find a place in the row of various helping professions, the question that is brought to their minds with an increasing urgency is: "What is there beyond professionalism—is ministry just another specialty in the many helping professions?" This question comes to the foreground again at a time when young students are questioning the value of the complicated distinctions between academic disciplines and are trying to come to terms with what is central and unifying in their lives.

During the last few years I have become overwhelmingly impressed by the fact that priests, ministers, and theological students who asked for supervision in their pastoral work were asking questions that went far beyond their professional concerns. In the beginning the emphasis quite often was on the best technique, the most appropriate method, the most effective approach: "How do I preach to a church congregation in a language that will make me understood? How can I be of help to a husband and wife struggling with marriage conflicts? How do I assist a dying patient? How do I behave when my community requires me to protest against the housing situation, wants me to work to alleviate poverty, or fight segregation and social injustice? Should I remain non-violent at all cost, or is there a time when violence might be the only ethical response?"

These questions are extremely important and call for intelligent discussions, careful research, and, often, long training under competent supervision.

But these questions are not the last ones and not the most decisive. Sometimes it even seems that underneath all these concerns is the question about the spirituality of the man or woman who raises them. Many students and trainees are struggling with their own sense of being. Long before they can ask themselves how to preach the gospel to others, they find themselves struggling with confusing questions: "Who is God to me? Does Jesus Christ really motivate my life?

How do I think about my own life and death? What do I really have to do with my neighbors? Is it my desire, task, or vocation to intervene in anyone's life at all? Should I speak about love when I question in my own heart that love is a possibility? Why read, talk, and teach about prayer when I never really experienced much of anything that deserves this title?"

These questions are not phrased in this very explicit way, but during the discussion of sermons, pastoral visits to sick people, religion classes, or any other ministerial task, I found that these questions are, knowingly or unknowingly, at the base of many frustrations for today's ministers. And if it is perhaps possible for a doctor to cure a patient even where the doctor hardly believes in the value of life, a Christian minister will never be able to be a minister if it is not his own most personal faith and insight into life that forms the core of his pastoral work.

So, ministry and spirituality never can be separated. Ministry is not an eight-to-five job but primarily a way of life, which is for others to see and understand so that liberation can become a possibility.

There is today a great hunger for a new spirituality that is a new experience of God in our own lives. This experience is essential for every minister but cannot be found outside of the limits of his ministry. It must be possible to find the seeds of this new spirituality right in the center of the Christian service. Prayer is not a preparation for work or an indispensable condition for effective ministry. Prayer is life; prayer and ministry are the same and can never be divorced. If they are, the minister becomes a handyman and the priesthood nothing more than another way to soften the many pains of daily life.

If the desire for silence, for moments of contemplation and meditation, is not born out of our concern for this world, we will soon become bored, not understanding why we have to be subjected to so many pious exercises. If God does not become more and more a living God to those who minister to the people of God every day, He will not be found in the desert, the convent, or the silent hours either. If professionalism is to be prevented from degenerating into a form of clerical manipulation, it has to be founded on the deep-rooted spiritual life of the minister himself as it develops out of his constant care for those he works with.

This is the main thrust of the following chapters. I hope to be able to show through the analysis of the five main functions of the ministry—teaching, preaching, individual pastoral care, organizing, and celebrating—the seeds of a spirituality for every man and woman who wants to be of service.

It will become clear that every Christian is a minister. The ordained ministry can be considered as a focus since the ordained minister gives the most visible shape to the different forms of Christian service. Therefore, the words "minister" and "priest" are often used in the following chapters. But what is true for ministers and priests in the formal sense is true for every man and woman who wants to live his life in the light of the Gospel of Jesus Christ. Therefore, in essence, this book is about the life-style of every Christian.

CREATIVE MINISTRY

CHAPTER I

BEYOND THE TRANSFERENCE OF KNOWLEDGE

TEACHING

INTRODUCTION

There was a time when God sent angels from heaven with an urgent message for man. He still does. A few months ago a Vietnamese Buddhist monk came to Holland and one day walked into the house where I lived. He was a thin, slender man whom you would be afraid to touch. But his clear, fearless eyes radiated an insight so deeply impregnated with affection that the only thing you could hope for was understanding. While he looked straight into my eyes he said: "There was a man on a horse galloping swiftly along the road. An old farmer standing in the fields, seeing him pass by, called out, 'Hey, rider, where are you going?' The rider turned around and shouted back, 'Don't ask me, just ask my horse!'"

The monk looked at me and said: "That is your condition. You are no longer master over your own destiny. You have lost control over the great powers that pull you forward toward an unknown direction. You have become a passive victim of an ongoing movement which you do not understand." It seemed as if he carved his message on my skin like a tattoo and then asked me to let it be seen wherever I go.

When we look at the situation of those who teach and those who are taught, the same question comes to mind: Do teachers and students really know where their horses are going?

Students are men and women who are supposed to be in the exceptional situation that allows them to reflect on themselves and their society under the guidance of competent teachers. They have set aside a certain amount of time in their lives to look explicitly at their own condition and at the condition of the world in which they live in the hope of being better able to understand and act accordingly.

But when we realize that today a "school" is no longer a "schola," which means free time, but has become a highly complex industry that prepares a man for an even more complex society, we might become receptive to the words of the Vietnamese Buddhist monk. If teaching means providing man with enough academic weapons to outdo his fellow man, to make more money, to have a better career, and more esteem in his neighborhood, we had better start asking ourselves if there is any word from God that supports this approach.

The most universal and most appreciated role of the Christian ministry through the ages has been teaching. Wherever Christians went to be of service, they always considered teaching as one of their primary tasks because of their conviction that increasing insight in man and his world is the way to new freedom and new ways of life. And although Christian churches frequently failed to live up to this conviction, even prevented the free growth of science and limited the fearless search for new fields of knowledge, they have always read in the Gospel a call to develop the human potentialities to the fullest through ongoing education.

The ministry of teaching has never limited itself, therefore, to the teaching of religion. Education is not primarily ministry because of what is taught but because of the nature of the educational process itself. Perhaps we have paid too much attention to the content of teaching without realizing that the teaching relationship is the most important factor in the ministry of teaching.

In this perspective, I raise the question: What do those who call themselves teachers or students really claim to be when they look at themselves in the light of the Gospel of Jesus Christ? In order to respond meaningfully to this question, I would like to describe two basic models of teaching —the violent model and the redemptive model—and then explicate the main resistances of man against learning.

By speaking in models, I will never do justice to individual teachers. I am not trying to. I only hope to map out basic structures that can help us to discover where we ourselves are and in which direction we want to go.

I. TEACHING AS A VIOLENT PROCESS

If we look at the overall educational situation today it seems as if students are constantly confronted with the complicated problems of their world and almost daily presented with new skills, methods, and techniques to get these problems under control. In fields like medicine, sociology, psychology, chemistry, biology, economics, and even theology, there is an amazing preoccupation with manipulative devices and the degree to which they satisfy immediate needs, relate to urgent problems, and keep an acceptable balance in the style of our lives. "Getting things under control" is what keeps most teachers and students busy, and a successful teacher is often the individual who creates the conviction that man has the

necessary tools to tame the dangerous lion he is going to
face as soon as he leaves the training field.

As long as teaching takes place in this context it is doomed
to be a violent process and evoke a vicious cycle of action
and reaction in which man faces his world as new territory
that has to be conquered but is filled with enemies unwilling
to be overruled by a stranger. The teacher who enters this
arena is forced to enter into a process which by its nature
is competitive, unilateral, and alienating. In short: violent.

Let us have a closer look at these three characteristics of
teaching as a violent process.

1. Competitive

Competition has become one of the most pervasive and also
destructive aspects of modern education. The way students
look at their fellow students and their teachers, the way
they expect their grades and degrees, the way they prepare
their exams and take them, the way they apply to college
and graduate school, and even the way in which they spend
their free time; all this and much more is impregnated by an
all-embracing sense of rivalry. You only have to walk during
the last week of a semester on a college campus to pick up
the mysterious A-B-C-D-and-F language that seems to be on
everyone's lips. The sadness of all this becomes clear when
you see that a student is only happy with a high grade when
he is sure that his fellow students have lower grades. It is
obvious that in a system that encourages this ongoing competition, knowledge no longer is a gift that should be shared,
but a property that should be defended.

Students who are aware of the fact that all their accomplishments, not only academic but athletic and social
accomplishments as well, will be compared with those of

others, and who realize that their grades will decide their further schooling, their future job, and even their military status, understandably can easily become victims of a paralyzing fear.

This fear makes many students oversensitive to the reaction of their friends and teachers. This fear makes them extremely self-conscious, highly defensive in their relationships with others, constantly concerned about the possibility of failure, and very hesitant to take any risks or do anything unexpected. Often this fear becomes the unaccepted ruler over everything they write, say, or even think. Through this fear, competition has become the great preventive in a student's free development of his total personality.

To show how deeply this competition has permeated the educational system, I would like to take a closer look at one of the teaching methods, which at first glance seems to be least competitive, the classroom discussion.

When you enter a college classroom today you will see that discussions have become an important part of modern education. The presupposition is that students learn more through discussion than through the absorption of ready-made information.

But is this always true? Quite often a closer analysis of an ongoing discussion shows that what in fact is happening is a sort of intellectual battle from which people tend to return more close-minded than when they entered it. Students sitting around the table, asking questions of their teacher, or phrasing their ideas and opinions before each other, are quite often more like soldiers charging with rifles than friends shaking hands.

Quite often the process goes like this: A student enters into the discussion without knowing much about the subject to be discussed, but with both a desire to know more about it and a fear of showing his ignorance. As soon as someone states an opinion, the most common reaction is not the internal question: "How can I understand *his* opinion better?" but "What is *my* opinion?" So, too, does silence often mean more an occasion to prepare an answer than to enter the train of thought of the other. And once two, three, or more opinions are stated the primary concern becomes defense of the chosen position, even when it is hardly worth defending. And so we see how after a while people try to convince themselves and others of ideas that in the beginning they hardly wanted to consider as their own—ideas that were only meant as a hesitant attempt to participate in an exchange of thoughts. And how could it be different when teachers are looked upon as those who are going to tell students, sooner or later, how much they are worth and when fellow-students are rivals in the big fight for academic survival? Who wants to be weak and vulnerable in such a situation? More importantly, who can really learn in this way?

2. *Unilateral*

The second characteristic of the violent form of teaching is that it is, in the final analysis, a unilateral process. Even the many discussion methods, which suggest that people learn from each other, can quite often be easily unmasked as simply more acceptable ways to get a definitive message across or to sell a so-called indispensable product. And when different forms of discussion prove to be not much more than cheap methods of advertisement, it is not so surprising that many students become quickly irritated by them, complain that they do not learn from them, and prefer straight lectures—which at least dispense with reading another book.

This all goes to say that underneath many methods of teaching is still the prevailing supposition that someone is competent and that someone else is not and that the whole game is to try to make the one just as or nearly as competent as the other. When this ideal is realized, the teacher is no longer considered as a teacher and the student as a student, and both can depart with not much more accomplished than the ability to tell stories about each other as an entertainment in their later years.

In this context the teacher is strong: He knows and should know. The student, however, is weak: He does not know and should want to know. The whole movement, therefore, is from teacher to student, from the strong to the weak, from one who knows to one who does not yet know. It is basically a unilateral process.

3. *Alienating*

Finally, the violent process of teaching is alienating because the eyes of the student are directed outwards, away from himself and his direct relationships into the future where the real things are supposed to happen to him. School, then, comes to be seen as only a preparation for later life, for the "real" life. One day the classroom will at last be left behind, the books will be closed, the teacher forgotten, and life can begin. School is just an indoor training, a dry-swim, a quasi life. It is not surprising, therefore, that many students are bored and tired during class and are killing time by anxiously waiting until the bell rings and they can start doing their own thing. Nor is it so strange that many say they have nothing or little to do with what happens at school and must go by blind faith that one day they will be thankful for the knowledge they received.

It is not so strange, then, that many teachers are looked upon as belonging to a world that is not the world of the students and that a hidden hostility often grows from this, expressing itself in a total lack of thankfulness towards those who have given much of their time, energy, and concern to prepare them for society.

This whole process is alienating because neither students nor teachers have been able to express their own individuality or use their regular relationships with each other as a primary source of learning. They have been pulled away from their own experiences; they are staring into the horizon expecting something to appear there, while at the same time they have become blind to what is happening right in front of them.

When many people spend about twenty years in school, it can be asked how valuable their lives have been if they should die at the end of those twenty years of life. Do those twenty years serve only as a preparation for another twenty years which, in their turn, have to make possible a final twenty years of retirement? But when a man does not really live here and now, why should he look forward to living somewhere else later? This is the core of alienation, a reality that is all too visible in the life of many students and teachers.

We have now described the violent process of teaching as one that is competitive, unilateral, and alienating. While it might never be found in its total naked destructiveness, it should, nonetheless, be clear that elements of it can be detected in many of our contemporary educational methods.

Now we are ready to look at an alternative model, which I have called "redemptive." I would hope that the foregoing elaboration has created the desire to hear more about it.

II.   TEACHING AS A REDEMPTIVE PROCESS

If it is true that in many instances we have become the passive victims of an educational process whose impact on us
we can hardly appreciate, it is imperative that we ask what
exactly it is that has happened to us. As my first general
impression, I suspect that we too often have lost contact with
the source of our own existence and have become strangers
in our own house. We tend to run around trying to solve
the problems of our world while anxiously avoiding con-
frontation with that reality wherein our problems find their
deepest roots: our own selves. In many ways we are like the
busy man who walks up to a precious flower and says: "What
for God's sake are you doing here? Can't you get busy
someway?" and then finds himself unable to understand the
flower's response: "I am sorry, sir, but I am just here to be
beautiful."

How can we also come to this wisdom of the flower that
being is more important than doing? How can we come to
a creative contact with the grounding of our own life? Only
through a teacher who can lead us to the source of our
existence by showing us who we are and, thereby, what
we are to do.

But where are these teachers? Some people think we have
lost our real teachers and live in a time without wise men.
But is that really so? Or should we say that there are no
teachers because there are no students? Teachers can only
become teachers when there are students who allow them to
be their teachers, and students can only become students
when there are teachers who allow them to be their students.
Only through this mutual acceptance can they enter into a

teacher-student relationship that can be described as redemptive. In contrast to the violent form of teaching—which is
competitive, unilateral, and alienating—therefore, the redemptive form of teaching can be described as evocative,
bilateral, and actualizing. Let us examine these characteristics
more closely.

1. Evocative

The first characteristic of a redemptive teacher-student relationship is that each tries to evoke in the other his respec-
tive potentials and make them available to each other. When
a student really wants to have a teacher he has to give someone the freedom to become his teacher by offering his own
life experiences as a source of insight and understanding.
Only the student who allows access into his own life experience can evoke in a man the possibility of becoming a real
teacher. In this sense the teacher depends completely on the
student, who has to give him his trust, confidence, and friendship, who has to share with him his weaknesses and strengths,
his desires and needs. Do not conclude too quickly that this
is unrealistic. There are, in fact, classrooms in which discussions become evocative forms of learning, and students are
able to offer their own experiences to their teachers and
fellow students in order to facilitate a deeper understanding.
In such cases, instead of the famous "Yes—but" dialogue,
you will hear "tell me more" or "that reminds me of" or
"to that I could add something." Competition is absent and
the teacher no longer is the fearful judge but the man to
whom is given the opportunity to be teacher and who can
invite the student to become more and more accessible to
learning. Perhaps no teacher can be a true teacher unless
he is also to a certain degree a friend. In other words, when
Christ said to His disciples: "I shall not call you servants
anymore, but friends" (John 15:14), He became in truth

their real teacher because all fear was overcome and real learning could begin.

2. Bilateral

The second characteristic of a redemptive teaching relationship is that it is bilateral. This means that not only the student has to learn from his teacher but, conversely, the teacher has to learn from his student. When the teacher is never willing to become student and to allow his student to be his teacher, he will never be able to make his teaching a redemptive process. Teachers and students are fellow men who together are searching for what is true, meaningful, and valid, and who give each other the chance to play each other's roles.

Few teachers, however, feel free enough to allow their students to know more than they, let alone to leave their students free enough to learn from them. They tend to think that they lose respect and esteem when they allow their students to guide them and, in so doing, fail to realize that it is exactly this freedom that will create the relationship by which they will be able to redeem the student from his fears and give him the freedom to grow. In this process, moreover, it is not so much the intellectual superiority of the teacher that counts as it is his maturity in facing the unknown and his willingness to leave unanswerable questions unanswered.

If the teaching process is a bilateral process, it is an essentially open-ended process. Discussion, therefore, is no longer a method to get a well-prepared opinion across to the student, but an exchange of experiences and ideas whose outcome is not determined. In this way, discussion might well lead to new and surprising perspectives and insights.

When teacher and students are willing to be influenced by each other, learning can become a creative process that can hardly be boring or tiring. It is only through a relationship of this sort that learning can take place.

3. *Actualizing*

This brings us to the third aspect of teaching as a redemptive process. It is not alienating but actualizing. This is to say that if learning is in some way to be a preparation for the future, it can only be so when the future becomes present in the teaching relationship here and now. To build a better world, the beginnings of that world must be visible in daily life. There is no reason to expect much to happen in the future if the signs of hope are not made visible in the present. We cannot speak about ways to bring about peace and freedom if we cannot draw from our own experiences of peace and freedom here and now. We cannot commit ourselves to work for justice and love in tomorrow's society if we cannot discover the seeds of it in the relationships we engage ourselves in today. A non-violent world cannot be born out of a violent teaching process any more than justice can be born out of jealousy, mildness out of cruelty, or love out of hate. But when schools are places where community can be experienced, where people can live together without fear of each other, and learning can be based on a creative exchange of experiences and ideas, then there is a chance that those who come from them will have an increasing desire to bring about in the world what they experienced during their years of formation. In this sense, schools are not training camps to prepare people to enter into a violent society but places where redemptive forms of society can be experimented with and offered to the modern world as alternative styles of life. Teaching then can become a way of creating a new life-style in which people are able to relate to each other in a basically non-violent way. And the teacher himself, in trying to live this way, will discover that learning itself is a way of life that goes far beyond the classroom situation, that it creates new relationships that do not finish when students leave, that it is a process that asks for continuation and is not limited by grades and degrees, and that it is a challenge to an ongoing renewal of one's style of life.

We have now described the redemptive process of teaching as an evocative, bilateral, and actualizing process. This ideal obviously never will be fully realized. But if we are able to realize at least the beginnings of it in our own situation, we might be encouraged to take the reins of the horse, into our hands and lead him away from violence in the direction of increasing freedom. Nonetheless, we would indeed be fooling ourselves if we thought the choice for a redemptive form of teaching was obvious. If this were the case, all the words written thus far would have been superfluous. The choice, however, is not obvious because we are faced with a deep-seated human resistance against learning. It is toward this resistance that we must now turn in order to both better understand it and thereby be able to remove it.

III. RESISTANCE AGAINST LEARNING

Learning is meant to lead to a redemptive insight into the condition of man and his world. But do we always desire insight? Bernard Lonergan writes:

> Just as insight can be desired, so too, it can be unwanted. Beside the love of light, there can be a love of darkness. If prepossessions and prejudices notoriously vitiate theoretical investigations, much more easily can

elementary passions bias understanding in practical and
personal matters. To exclude an insight is also to exclude
the further questions that would arise from it and the
complementary insights that would carry it towards a
rounded and balanced viewpoint. To lack that fuller
view results in behavior that generates misunderstand-
ing both in ourselves and in others. To suffer such
incomprehension favours a withdrawal from the outer
drama of human living into the inner drama of phan-
tasy.

(*Insight*, Longmans Green and Co., Ltd.,
London, 1957, p. 191.)

Lonergan calls such an aberration of understanding a
"scotosis," derived from the Greek word, *skotos*, which
means darkness, and the resultant blind spot a "scotoma."
By introducing these terms, he has helped us to come to
a better understanding of the massive resistance against learning. For it is exactly this scotosis that prevents us from
really dealing with those factors that are crucial today in
man's making of himself. By this scotosis, this exclusion of
painful insights, we prevent our own experience from becoming part of the learning process and become like un-
engaged spectators in the procession of life.

I am trying to say very simple and obvious things here.
But if it is true that the most obvious things can easily
become the most threatening things to us, then perhaps
they also can become the easiest subjects of scotosis.

Scotosis means long and fierce discussions about justice
and equality while we hate our teacher or ignore the needs
of our fellow students. Scotosis means endless academic
quarrels in a world filled with atrocities and much talk
about hunger by people suffering from overweight. Scotosis
allows church people to indulge in comfortable discussions
about the Kingdom of God while they should know that

God is with the poor, the sick, the hungry, and the dying. In Lonergan's words: "Scotosis means an aberration which prevents the emergence into consciousness of perspectives that would give rise to unwanted insights" (op. cit., p. 192). It is indeed startling to discover how we keep ourselves free from those unwanted insights.

Why is this scotosis so difficult to heal? What keeps us blind to the obvious? If we could find some answers to these questions, we could begin, at least in part, to understand why there is such a powerful resistance to learning and why it is so difficult for teaching to become a redemptive process.

I would like to suggest three reasons that keep us from learning and at the same time might explain many of our teacher-student scotomas: 1) a wrong supposition, 2) a false pressure, and 3) a horror of self-encounter.

1. A wrong supposition

Many teachers as well as many students still operate under the faulty supposition that it is better to give than to receive. Teachers want to give something to students—an idea, an opinion, a specific skill, advice, or any other thing they think students are waiting for—and students, in turn, value their teachers according to what they have to give.

It is difficult to recognize the meaning of Christ's saying: "There is more happiness in giving than in receiving" (Acts 20:35), because it is difficult to confess that perhaps the greatest service we can offer to our fellow man is to receive and allow *him* the happiness of giving. For much of the happiness in our lives is derived from the fact that we can give and that our friends have been willing to receive our gifts, to make them a part of their lives, and to allow themselves to become dependent on us through them. We feel happy when we see the picture we gave our friend displayed most advantageously on a wall of his living room. The question is: Would we have given him the freedom to put it in the attic?

A gift only becomes a gift when it is received; and nothing we have to give—wealth, talents, competence, or just beauty—will ever be recognized as true gifts until someone opens his hands or heart to accept them.

This all suggests that he who wants someone else to grow —that is to discover his potential and capacities, to experience that he has something to live and work for—should first of all be able to recognize that person's gifts and be willing to receive them. For man only becomes fully man when he is received and accepted. In this way, many students could be better students than they actually are if there were someone who could make them recognize their capacities and could accept these as a real gift to him. Students grow during those moments in which they discover they have offered something new to their teachers without making them feel threatened but, rather, thankful. And teachers could be much better teachers if students were willing to draw the best out of them and show their acceptance by thankfulness and creative work. Too many people cling to their own talents and leave them untouched because they are afraid there is nobody who is really interested. They then regress into their own fantasies and suffer from a growing loss of self-esteem.

As long as we keep living with the wrong supposition that giving is our first task, our scotosis cannot be healed, and the most creative insights will stay out of our consciousness.

2. *False pressure*

A second reason that prevents our scotosis from healing is that we are caught in the deadly network of a modern educational process, which makes us believe we are better and more competent men when we have better grades, higher degrees, and more academic rewards. A great many hours are spent by both teachers and students in trying to keep up with the physically and mentally exhausting routine of academic life. We have put such a high value on degrees and certificates that we are willing to trust ourselves blindly to a man with an M.D. or a Ph.D. who, a few months earlier when he was still struggling for his exams, we were more inclined to qualify as one of those irresponsible rebellious students.

This false pressure of society, which forces us to pay undue attention to the formal recognition of our intellectual accomplishments, tends to pull us away from our own more personal needs and to prevent us from coming to insights into our own experiences that can form the basis of a creative life project.

3. *Horror of self-encounter*

The final and most powerful resistance against learning, however, is much deeper and much more profound. It is the resistance against a conversion that calls for a "kenotic" self-encounter. We will only be able to be creatively receptive and break through the imprisoning strings of academic conformity when we can squarely face our fundamental human condition and fully experience it as the foundation of all learning in which both students and teachers are

involved. It is the experience that teacher and student are
both sharing the same reality—that is, they are both naked,
powerless, destined to die, and, in the final analysis, totally
alone and unable to save each other or anyone else. It is
the embarrassing discovery of solidarity in weakness and of
a desperate need to be liberated from slavery. It is the
confession that they both live in a world filled with unreali-
ties and that they allow themselves to be driven by the most
trivial desires and the most distasteful ambitions.

Only if students and teachers are willing to face this painful reality can they free themselves for real learning. For only
in the depths of his loneliness, when he has nothing to
lose any more and does not cling any longer to life as to an
inalienable property, can a man become sensitive to what
really is happening in his world and be able to approach
it without fear.

This conversion, which is not a sudden event but an ongoing process, is the most important prerequisite for arriv-
ing at redemptive insights and removing our many blind
spots.

So we have seen how a wrong supposition, false pressure,
and horror for self-encounter make it extremely difficult to
heal our scotosis, to take away our resistance against learning,
and to make a redemptive form of teaching a real possibility.

CONCLUSION

The core idea of this chapter has been that ultimately we
can only come from a violent form of teaching to a redemp-

tive form of teaching through a conversion that pervades our total personality and breaks the power of our resistance against learning.

Jesus can be called Teacher in the fullest sense of the word precisely because He did not cling to His prerogatives but became one of the many who have to learn. His life makes it clear to us that we do not need weapons, that we do not need to hide ourselves or play competitive games with each other. Only he who is not afraid to show his weaknesses and who allows himself to be touched by the tender hand of the Teacher will be able to be a real student. For if education is meant to challenge the world, it is Christ Himself who challenges teachers as well as students to give up their defenses and to become available for real growth. In order to come to this conversion, which is the healing of our scotomas, we might be thrown from our horses and be blind for a while, but in the end we will be brought to an entirely new insight, which might well bring about a new man in a new world.

CHAPTER II

BEYOND THE RETELLING OF THE STORY

PREACHING

INTRODUCTION

In 1857 Anthony Trollope wrote in *Barchester Towers:*
"There is, perhaps, no greater hardship at present inflicted
on mankind in civilised and free countries, than the necessity of listening to sermons." (cf., *U. S. Catholic,* July 1970,
"Let's Abolish the Sunday Sermon," by Daphne D. C.
Pochin Mould.) I would not be surprised to find many
people today who are willing to agree with him.

The more amazing it is, therefore, that there are still
so many preachers who want to preach and so many people
who are willing to listen. Why is this so? Perhaps because
people today, just as much as a century ago, have a lasting
desire to come to such an insight in their own condition
and the condition of their world, they can be free to follow
Christ: that is, to live their lives just as authentically as
He lived His. The purpose of preaching is none other
than to help man to come to this basic insight.

Insight is more than intellectual understanding—it is
knowledge through and through, knowledge to which the
whole person can say Yes. It is an understanding that pervades man from head to heart, from top to toe, from brain
to guts. When a man can come to this totally permeating
knowledge, he will be able to really listen to the Word of

God and to follow the light that entered into his darkness. In this way, one of the most crucial purposes of preaching is to remove these real and all-too-visible obstacles that cause man to listen without understanding.

Not too long ago during Sunday Mass in a Dutch church, a friend of mine gave a sermon on which he had spent at least three days of preparation. After the service I saw a seventeen-year-old boy sitting in the last pew. Since I had helped my friend with his sermon, I was curious to find out how people felt about it. So I walked over to the boy and said: "Say, how did you like that sermon?" He looked at me as if I could not have asked a sillier question, brushed his hair away from his eyes, and said: "Sir, I never listen to sermons. That is the time when I take my nap." Somewhat thrown off balance by his response, I looked around to find someone who could give me a little more support. When I saw a man, in his thirties, walking out of the church with his wife and children, I stopped him, saying: "Mister, can I ask you a question? What did you think about the sermon today." He immediately responded: "Well—that priest certainly looked like a nice young man —but I think he still has a lot to learn. All that talk about Camillo Torres and Martin Luther King—and that we all should help to change the church—You know, sir? I wish they would let *me* get up on that pulpit and say something. Sometimes my hands are just itching and I am about to stand up and say something back—but my wife feels that I say enough at home and should at least be quiet in church."

The boy's indifference and the man's irritation are two reactions to preaching that prevent many people from listening to those ministers and priests who are trying their best to reach the hundreds of people still willing to visit their churches on Sunday. If insight is the purpose of preaching, and if indifference and irritation are two of the main obstacles that confront it, we find ourselves right in the middle of the problem of preaching.

Preaching belongs to the heart of the Christian ministry. Historians, systematic theologians, and especially biblical scholars—all have many contributions to offer for a better understanding of this crucial ministerial task. It would, however, be extremely presumptuous to even try to touch the many aspects of preaching. Therefore, I would like to limit myself to just one question: "What kind of man is it who can help take away those obstacles that prevent the Word of God from falling on fertile ground?"

The question is really a question about the spirituality of the preacher. But before we can realistically approach it, we must first take a close look at two of the main difficulties in preaching: One is in the message itself, the other is in the messenger. Therefore, I would like to divide this chapter into three parts: 1) the problem of the message, 2) the problem of the messenger, and 3) the man who can lead to insight.

I. THE PROBLEM OF THE MESSAGE

In order to bring any kind of message to people there has to be at least the willingness to accept the message. This willingness means some desire to listen, some question that asks for an answer, or some general feeling of uncertainty that needs clarification or understanding. But whenever an answer is given when there is no question, support is offered when there is no need, or an idea is given when there is

no desire to know, the only possible effect can be irritation or
plain indifference.

It is no secret that those who address themselves to people
in church find quite often that the number of people present
is in direct opposition to the eagerness to listen. And when
teachers and lecturers express a certain jealousy in regard
to the many people who come under the influence of a
preacher, they tend to forget that there are few audiences
that are so little motivated to listen as a church congregation.
What causes this lack of motivation? I suspect there are
two aspects of the message that can explain at least part
of this phenomenon: 1) the redundancy of the message
and 2) the fearfulness of the message.

1.   The redundancy of the message

If we say that preaching means announcing the good news,
it is important to realize that for most people there is absolutely no news in the sermon. Practically nobody listens
to a sermon with the expectation of hearing something they
did not already know. They have heard about Jesus—His
disciples, His savings, His miracles, His death and resur-
rection—at home, in kindergarten, in grade school, in high
school, and in college so often and in so many different
ways and forms that the last thing they expect to come from
a pulpit is any news. And the core of the Gospel—"You
must love the Lord your God with all your heart, with all
your soul, and with all your mind and you must love your
neighbor as yourself"—has been repeated so often and so
persistently that it has lost, for the majority of people,
even the slightest possibility of evoking any response.
They have heard it from the time of their earliest childhood
and will continue to hear it until they are dead—unless,

of course, they become so bored on the way that they refuse
to place themselves any longer in a situation in which they
will be exposed to this redundant information. It is fascinat-
ing to see how people sit up straight, eyes wide open, when
the preacher starts his sermon with a little secular story by
way of appetizer, but immediately turn on their sleeping
signs and curl up in a more comfortable position when the
famous line comes: "And this, my brothers and sisters, is
exactly what Jesus meant when He said . . ." From then on
most preachers are alone, relying only on the volume of
their voices or the idiosyncrasies of their movements to keep
in contact. It is indeed sad to say that the name of Jesus
for many people has lost most of its mobilizing power. Too
often the situation is like the one in the Catholic school
where the teacher asked: "Children, who invented the steam
engine?" Everyone was silent until finally a little boy sitting
in the back of the class raised his finger and said in a dull
voice and with watery eyes: "I guess it is Jesus again."

When a message has become so redundant that it has
completely lost the ability to evoke any kind of creative response it can hardly be considered a message any longer. And
if you feel you cannot avoid being present physically at its
presentation you at least can close your eyes and mind and
drop out.

2. The fearfulness of the message

But redundancy is only one aspect of the message that prevents people from listening. And even though it may be
realistic to admit that there is hardly any news in the sermon
for most people, the core message of the Gospel nonetheless
contains a Truth that no one has yet fully made true. And
real listening means nothing less than the constant willingness to confess that you have not yet realized what you

profess to believe. Who likes to hear, for example, that the last will be first, if he happens to be first? And who wants to hear that those who are poor, who mourn, who are hungry, thirsty, and persecuted are called happy, when he is wealthy, self-content, well-fed, praised for his good wines, and admired by all his friends? Who wants to hear that he has to love his enemies and pray for those who persecute him when he calls his boss an S.O.B., his own son a good-for-nothing tramp, and glows with pride when he reads that the boys in Vietnam have bagged another few hundred V.C.s. The message might be the same all through life and might be repeated over and over again in different words and styles, but he who will let it really come through allows himself, at the same time, the possibility of coming to an insight that might well have consequences for his style of life, which he is not eager to take. The truth, after all, is radical: It goes to the roots of a man's life in such a way that few are those who want it and the freedom it brings with it. There is, in fact, such an outright fear to face the Truth in all its directness and simplicity that irritation and anger seem to be a more common human response than a humble confession that one also belongs to the group Jesus criticized. In this way, many breakfast discussions on Sunday are, for example, nothing less than clear-cut attempts to undo any possible effects of the threatening Truth. When someone says, "I wish I could get up there and tell those priests how life is when you're married and have three kids," he is often expressing what is in fact a deep-seated resistance to confess that the Gospel is also speaking to a man with a family. And just as indifference can make a man unavailable for the word of the Gospel, so too can irritation bar the way for new and liberating insights.

Redundancy of the message and fear of the Truth seem to be the two basic reasons why a preacher has such difficulty in coming close to his audience. This is perhaps even more the case when those who are present scarcely feel free to walk out. Many still feel bound to some far authority from Heaven, from Rome, or from the chancellery who has convinced them that if they are unwilling to suffer one hour a week, they will surely suffer a great deal more when all their weeks have passed. As a result, a preacher is again facing an extremely hard task: To proclaim the good news, which for many is neither new nor good.

Before we can ask what kind of man will be able to break through this deep-seated human resistance against the message, we have to be honest enough to confess that it is not just the message but also the messenger himself who often keeps men away from painful but liberating insights. Let us, therefore, now examine the problem of the messenger.

II. THE PROBLEM OF THE MESSENGER

Many preachers tend to increase the resistance against listening instead of decreasing it by the way in which they tend to get their eternal message across. A critical analysis of many sermons would show that if the Prophet Isaiah was correct when he said: "You will listen and not understand, see—and not perceive" (Isaiah 6:9–10), many preachers certainly do not help to allow a few exceptions to his prophecy. It would prove useful, then, to have a closer look at a few ways of preaching that might make us better understand the problem of the messenger. In this regard I would suggest that the two main reasons why a preacher often creates more antagonism than sympathy are: 1) the assumption of non-existent feelings and 2) the preoccupation with a theological point of view.

1. *Non-existent feelings*

A large number of sermons start by making untested suppositions. Without any hesitance, many preachers impose feelings, ideas, questions, and problems on their hearers that are often completely unknown to the majority, if not to all of them. Some preachers make their hearers ask themselves why their chasubles are red on Pentecost, why the last Sunday of the liturgical year is not in December, why Lent lasts forty days, why All Souls Day is immediately after All Saints Day—questions about which people could not care less and which are usually left-over problems from the priest's own vague memories of the volumes of Pius Parsh.

Sometimes whole sermons are built on clerical feelings that are quite alien to laymen. I remember one sermon that began as follows:

> Today we all congregate together to celebrate the ascension of our Lord Jesus Christ. Only a few weeks ago our hearts were still filled with joy because of the resurrection of our Lord, and now already we feel with the Apostles the sadness about His leaving us. But let us not despair, because Jesus does not leave us alone but is going to send us the Holy Spirit within a few days. And not only for the Apostles but also for this community gathered around His altar the Spirit will bring new life and new hope—

It came as no surprise to find that everyone was mentally absent by the time the preacher finished his introduction. I counted about thirty people scattered in the big, mostly empty, church. Nobody seemed to remember how happy he was at Easter or to realize how sad he was on Ascension Day. There was no congregation, no celebration, no com-

munity, certainly no despair or desire to have the Holy
Spirit come soon. Just a couple of isolated individuals who
had kept in mind that Ascension Day is a day of obligation
and were faithful enough to go to Mass.

Even more irritating than this, however, are preachers who
somehow seem to know exactly how everybody feels. A
good example is the following introduction:

> Brothers and Sisters in Christ,
>
> In a time in which we all have become part of the big
> American rat race, in which we are forced to become
> victims of our watches and slaves of our agendas, in
> which we are running from one committee meeting to
> another, we have become deaf to the voice of God who
> speaks in silence and reveals himself in the quiet mo-
> ments of prayer.

Well, this certainly tells us a lot about the preacher—but
what about the grandmother who spent a good part of the
week solving crossword puzzles, what about the boy who
just came back from the baseball field, and his teacher
who spent his free Saturday reading Dostoyevsky, and what
about the housewife who enjoyed a nice afternoon with
her kids at the city zoo?

Perhaps someone in the audience might say Yes to the
preacher, but most will feel just as far from his words
as they feel from the so-called rat race. They might not
be aware of this, but in one way or another—by a protective
numbness or an outright expression of hostility—they will
show that they are not really with him.

2. *Theological preoccupation*

A second and even more difficult problem to overcome is
the theological preoccupation of the preacher. Some preach-

ers become so excited about a recent book they have read
or a new viewpoint they have heard that they feel com-
pelled to have others share their enthusiasm. They quickly
and, as it often happens, disappointingly find out, however,
that Karl Rahner, Harvey Cox, or Schillebeeckx do not
appeal as much, if at all, to their hearers as they do to
themselves. The main reason is not that their theological
ideas are not valid or meaningful, but rather that not only
those who preach but also those who listen have their own
"theologies." Let me explain this with a story.

A theology student was asked to give a sermon about the
Kingdom of God. He carefully studied the Scriptures and
read the latest literature on the subject. But when he thought
he had a clear idea about the Kingdom of God and was
ready to present his sermon, the suggestion was made to
him to first visit four families living in the parish where
he was going to preach and ask them what they thought
about the Kingdom of God.

So he went first to a meteorologist, a scholarly man who
had read many books in his life and had discovered that
making predictions was a pretty tricky business. And the
meteorologist said: "The Kingdom of God is the fulfillment
of God's promises, and man has to refrain from the un-
healthy curiosity of exactly how this will happen."

Then the student went to a storekeeper, whose business
had been a failure and whose wife had been sick for many
years. And the storekeeper said: "The Kingdom of God is
heaven—where I finally will receive my reward for enduring
my hard, bothersome life."

From the storekeeper he went to a wealthy farmer, who
had a strong wife and two beautiful and healthy children.
And the farmer said: "The Kingdom of God is a beautiful

garden where we all will continue the happy life we started in this world."

Finally, the student came to the house of a laborer, who had learned a good trade and was proud that he was able to earn his money with his own hands. And the laborer said: "The Kingdom of God was a smart invention of the Church to keep the illiterate happy and the poor content, but since I can take care of myself and have a good job I have no need any more for a kingdom to come."

When the theology student came home from his visits and read his sermon again, he realized suddenly that his ideas were close to those of the meteorologist, who was used to living with uncertainties, but that the storekeeper looking for a reward, the farmer hoping for the continuation of his happiness, and the laborer who saw the Kingdom in the works of his own hands would not understand him. And when he read the Scriptures again he discovered that there was a place for all four of his parishioners in the Kingdom of God. (These data are used with the permission of Mr. Leo Lans, student of Catholic Theological Institute in Utrecht, Holland.)

Perhaps the greatest temptation of the preacher is to think that only he has a theology and to believe that the best thing to do is to convert all those who listen to his way of thinking. In this way, however, he has failed to realize that in a very real sense he has not loved his neighbor as himself, since he has not taken their views and experiences just as seriously as his own. When this is true, in fact, many of those who listen to his viewpoint will become indifferent or irritated without exactly knowing why. And the preacher who spends a great deal of time studying books and preparing his sermons will himself become more and more disillusioned as he starts feeling that nobody wants to listen to the Word of God. All the while, however, he has forgotten that God's Word does not have to be exactly the same as his own. When the preacher addresses himself to non-existent feelings and is anxiously preoccupied with his own theology, he tends to increase instead of decrease the already existing resistance against the message.

At this point one might well be inclined to ask how the preacher can overcome this problem. From the outset, however, we have to say that the question itself is misdirected, for there is no tool, no technique, no special skill which can solve the preacher's problem. But perhaps there is a "spirituality"—a way of living—that can give hope to the man who wants to bring his people to a liberating insight which can make them free to follow Christ. Let us, therefore, now examine the kind of man who can help others to come to this insight.

III. THE MAN WHO LEADS TO INSIGHT

The task of every preacher is to assist men in their ongoing struggle of becoming. And this is accomplished primarily by speaking about Christ, Who lived His life with an increasing willingness to face His own condition and the condition of the world in which He found Himself, in such a way that man is encouraged to follow Him; that is, to live his life with the same authenticity even if it leads him to tears, sweat, and possibly, a violent death.

Every preacher is called upon to take away the obstacles that prevent this painful process of man's becoming man. This is a difficult task since there seems to be a profound resistance in man against change, at least when it concerns his basic outlook on life. Once we have a more or less satisfying standpoint, we tend to cling to it since it always seems better to have at least a poor standpoint than to have none at all. In this sense man is basically very conservative. He is constantly tempted to deny his most precious human ability—which is to shift standpoints—and yields easily to his tendency to settle for the comfortable routine. In many ways he is resistant to the call of Him Who says that when you are young you can put on your own belt and walk where you like, but when you grow old you will stretch your hands and somebody else will put a belt round you and take you where you would rather not go (John 21:18). In complete contrast to our idea that adulthood means the ability to take care of oneself, Jesus describes it as a growing willingness to stretch out one's hands and be guided by others.

It is no wonder, then, that a preacher who hopes to remove the obstacles of this process of growth and to have his people become free to surrender themselves and let others gird them is considered a man with great courage.

The two aspects of preaching that seem to be most essential for a preacher to facilitate this ongoing process of becoming are: 1) dialogue and 2) availability.

1. The capacity for dialogue

When I use the word dialogue I do not think about dialogue homilies in which everyone can say what he wants, nor about a public discussion or any other specific technique to make people participate. No, nothing of that is meant by the word dialogue. I simply mean a way of relating to men and women so that they are able to respond to what is said with their own life experience. In this way dialogue is not a technique but an attitude of the preacher who is willing to enter into a relationship in which partners can really influence each other. In a true dialogue the preacher cannot stay on the outside. He cannot remain untouchable and invulnerable. He has to be totally and most personally involved. This can be a completely internal process in which there is no verbal exchange of words, but it requires the risk of real engagement in the relationship between he who speaks and those who listen. Only then can we talk about a real dialogue.

When this dialogue takes place, those who listen will come to the recognition of who they really are since the words of the preacher will find a sounding board in their own hearts and find anchor places in their personal life-experiences. And when they allow his words to come so close as to become their flesh and blood, they can say: "What you say loudly, I whispered in the dark; what you pronounce so clearly, I had some suspicion about; what you put in the foreground, I felt in the back of my mind; what you hold so firmly in your hand always slipped away through my fingers. Yes, I find myself in your words because your words come from the depths of human experiences and, therefore, are not just yours but also mine, and your insights do not just belong to you, but are mine as well."

When a man who listens to a preacher can say this, there is a real dialogue. And if he were a little more spontaneous than most of us are, he would say, "Yes, brother, you said it. Yes, Amen Alleluia." Only then is man able to recognize real dialogue and affirm his real self and come to the confession not only of his deficiencies and mistakes but also of himself as a man in desperate need for the Word of God which has the power to make him free. But when man is not able to understand what is going on within himself, when he does not know what he really wants, feels, or does, then words that come from above cannot penetrate into the center of his person. When emotions, ideas, and aspirations are cluttered together in an impermeable dirty crust, no dew can bring forth fruits and no clouds can "rain the just."

But whenever the anxious and impenetrable man is approached by a fellow man who expresses his solidarity with him and offers his insight and understanding as a source of recognition and clarification, then his confusion can be taken away and paths that may lead to light can become visible. Then the meteorologist, the storekeeper, the farmer, and the laborer will realize that the man up there is simply taking away the veil that prevented them from seeing not his but their own viewpoints. Then they will recognize that he is speaking about them and that the Word of God is not for him alone.

A beautiful example of this dialogue is the sermon given by William Sloane Coffin, Jr., in Battell Chapel in New Haven, Connecticut, on April 10, 1970, during the days of the Panther trial. He started this sermon with the following words:

> Most of us who are here today are in deep distress. The Panther trial is polarising not only our Yale-New Haven community and increasingly the entire nation; it is also polarising ourselves. The innermost feelings of many of us are now so sharply divided that they are destroying our capacity to think and act with anything approaching conviction and compassion.
> (*Yale Daily News,* Monday, April 20, 1970.)

That is dialogue, and because many in Coffin's audience could say Yes, they recognized their own paralysis, and this recognition created their first desire to move again and do something. The words of Coffin that followed were so extremely effective because his hearers were ready for them. It is no surprise that this sermon was an important contribution to the creative response to the fearful situation in New Haven.

But again, dialogue is not a technique or a special skill you can learn in school, but a way of life. Nobody can imitate Coffin or any other effective preacher. In the final analysis, dialogue can only become actual through a willingness on the part of the preacher to be available to his audience in a very basic sense. And so, I would finally like to examine this availability as the core of the spirituality of the preacher.

2. *Availability*

Availability is the primary condition for every dialogue that is to lead to a redemptive insight. A preacher who is not willing to make his understanding of his own faith and doubt, anxiety and hope, fear and joy available as a source of recognition for others can never expect to remove the many obstacles which prevent the Word of God from bearing fruit.

But it is here that we touch precisely upon the spirituality of the preacher himself. In order to be available to others, a man has to be available to himself first of all. And we know how extremely difficult it is to be available to ourselves, to have our own experiences at our disposal. We know how selective our self-understanding really is. If we are optimists, we are apt to remember those events of the day that tend to reinforce our positive outlook on life. If we are pessimists, we might say to ourselves: "Again, another day that proves that I am no good." But where is the realist who is able to allow all his experiences to be his, and to accept his happiness as well as his sadness, his hate as well as his love, as really belonging to his own human experiences? When a man does not have all his experiences at his disposal he tends to make only those available to others that fit best the image he wants to have of himself and his world. And this is exactly what we call "close-mindedness." It is the blindness of a man to an essential part of his own reality.

A preacher who wants to be a real leader is the man who is able to put the full range of his life-experiences— his experiences in prayer, in conversation and in his lonely hours—at the disposal of those who ask him to be their preacher. Pastoral care does not mean running around nervously trying to redeem people, to save them at the last moment, or to put them on the right track by a good idea, an intelligent remark, or practical advice. No! Man is redeemed once and for all. Pastoral care means in the final analysis: offering your own life-experience to your fellow man and, as Paul Simon sings, to lay yourself down like a bridge over troubled water.

I am not saying that you should talk about yourself, your personal worries, your family, your youth, your illnesses, or your hang-ups. That has nothing to do with availability. That is only playing a narcissistic game with your own idiosyncrasies. No, I mean that a preacher is called to experience life to such a depth that the meteorologist, the storekeeper, the farmer, and the laborer will all one day or another realize that he is touching places where their own lives also really vibrate, and in this way he allows them to become free to let the Word of God do its redemptive work. Because, as Carl Rogers says: "What is most personal is most general." (*On Becoming a Person*, Houghton Mifflin, New York, 1961, p. 26.) Thomas Oden explains this when he writes: "Repeatedly I have found, to my astonishment, that the feelings which have seemed to me most private, most personal,

and therefore the feelings I least expect to be understood by
others, when clearly expressed, resonate deeply and consist-
ently with their own experience. This has led me to believe
that what I experience in the most unique and personal way,
if brought to clear expression, is precisely what others are
most deeply experiencing in analogous ways." (*The Structure
of Awareness,* Abingdon Press, Nashville and New York,
1969, pp. 23–24.)

When a man listens to a preacher who is really available
to himself and, therefore, able to offer his own life experience
as a source of recognition, he no longer has to be afraid to
face his own condition and that of his world because the
one who stands in front of him is the living witness that
insight makes him free and does not create new anxieties.
Only then can indifference and irritation be removed, only
then can the Word of God, which has been repeated so often
but understood so little, find fertile ground and be rooted in
the soul of man.

So we have seen how, through availability, a real dialogue
can take place which can lead to new insight. This is to
say that the Word of God, which is a sign of contradiction
and a sword piercing the heart of man, can only reach
people when it has become the flesh and blood of him who
preaches it.

CONCLUSION

I have used a lot of words to say a very simple thing: A
preacher is a man who is willing to give his life for his people.
The Word of God is always coming into the world, though
it is often met with indifference and irritation. He who

preaches is called upon to remove these obstacles and lead men to a true insight that can set them free.

If the preacher does not want to increase the resistance against the Word but decrease it, he has to be willing to lay himself down and make his own suffering and his own hope available to others so that they too can find their own, often difficult way. Nobody can ever claim to be a real preacher in this sense. Only Christ could, since only He entered into a full dialogue with those He loved by laying down His life in total availability. But out of all those who witnessed His death and saw the blood and water come from His pierced side, only a few were willing to cast off their indifference and irritation and come to the liberating insight: "In truth this was the son of God" (Mt. 27:54).

Every time real preaching occurs the crucifixion is realized again: for no preacher can bring anyone to the light without having entered the darkness of the Cross himself. Perhaps Anthony Trollope was right when he said that the necessity of listening to semons is the greatest hardship inflicted on mankind in civilized and free countries. But if we want our countries to become really free and civilized, let us hope that there always will be men to endure the hardship of preaching and lead their people through their own darkness to the Light of God.

CHAPTER III

BEYOND THE SKILLFUL RESPONSE

INDIVIDUAL PASTORAL CARE

INTRODUCTION

In order to deal concretely and specifically with the relationship between individual pastoral care and the spirituality of the minister, I would like to start this chapter with the story of Michael Smith, a pastoral trainee in Stone Memorial Hospital. The head of the section where Michael was working told him that one of the patients, Mr. Kern, had cancer and was in very critical condition, and that a visit might be worthwhile.

Michael, dressed in a white coat like the medical interns but with a name tag identifying him as a chaplain, entered Mr. Kern's room for a pastoral visit. There the following conversation took place:

Mr. Kern: You're a new one. I don't believe I've seen you among the doctors.

Michael: You haven't, I'm sure, though I have been meaning to call on you sooner. I should have been here sooner than this. I am one of the chaplains, Chaplain Smith.

Mr. Kern: How do you do.

Michael: I just want to say Hello to you. I want to let you know that we're around and that we'll be happy to help in any way we can. The chaplain's office answers on extension 2765, and in case you are interested, there are services here on Sunday—several ecumenical and one Mass for Catholics.

Mr. Kern: I am Jewish.

Michael: Oh, fine. In that event you may be interested to know that though he is not here daily, a Rabbi makes regular visits here at Stone Memorial. Could I call him for you?

Mr. Kern: Please do not. I would prefer not to bother him—or anyone.

Michael: If you wish—How ill have you been?

Mr. Kern: Enough to die, but I don't! And all this doctoring has done and does no good—a continual torture. But I do not care to talk. Will you please excuse me?

Michael: I'm sure that I have come in at a very inopportune time, and I hope that I have not disturbed or upset you. Still, I would like to drop in from time to time, if for no other reason than to say Hello, just to see how things are with you.

Mr. Kern: You would indeed be doing me a very great favor—and would be respecting my wishes perfectly, as I have told the doctors—if you and everyone else would leave me entirely alone. My own family, except for my wife, does not come to see me. I have told my daughter not to come. I don't want her to see me in this condition. Yet people insist. Even a dying animal—a dying animal—can crawl off by itself to die. I repeat: You will be doing me a favor if you leave—and do not return.

Back at his room Michael wrote: "I feel discouraged, even guilty. It was almost as if I had been kicked in the stomach."

(This case is used with the permission of Dr. Seward Hiltner of Princeton Theological Seminary.)

This painful visit and the even more painful reflection on it raises three questions that have been raised over and over again in respect to individual pastoral care.

1. Who are you, Michael, to visit Mr. Kern?
2. What kind of relationship do you expect to have with this patient?
3. What do you think you can do for him?

These three questions refer to the pastoral identity, the pastoral relationship, and the pastoral approach. In recent years many ministers and priests have been involved in special training programs in order to become more adept at serving the individual needs of their fellow men. Under the guidance of competent supervisors and with the help of new insights in psychodynamics and especially psychotherapy, many have been working hard to make their ministry relevant to men and women struggling with the meaning of their lives and their deaths. But while concentrating on their own identity, or the relationships they have with people, and the help they can offer, many ministers and priests begin to realize the far-reaching implications for their own most personal life. It is these implications for the spirituality of the minister that I would like to discuss here.

We will divide this chapter into three parts: Spirituality and the pastoral identity, Spirituality and the pastoral relationship, Spirituality and the pastoral approach.

I. SPIRITUALITY AND PASTORAL IDENTITY

The first question Michael Smith had to face is: Who am I? He is not a doctor on the hospital staff who is expected to cure Mr. Kern of his cancer, he is not a psychologist trained to help Mr. Kern cope with his anxieties, he is not a social worker able to see just how far the relationship with his wife and daughters can be of any support to Mr. Kern. What, then, is his specialty, his own unique contribution, his most personal tool?

The question is a very realistic one in a world that is becoming more and more professionalized and where one specialty after another is developing. There was a time in which the minister indeed was doctor, psychologist, social worker, and nurse all at once, and in which he was the factotum of the community, the center of knowledge and wisdom. But today many ministers feel that they are amateurs in every field and professional in none. And in the middle of this confusion they often feel very inadequate, suffer from a painfully low self-esteem, and doubt if their theology can be made operational to such a degree that people can be helped in an effective way.

It seems that there are two sides to the pastoral identity which demand careful attention:

1. *Self-affirmation*

After the visit to Mr. Kern, Michael found himself discouraged and guilty. He felt that he had imposed himself on someone who had neither asked for nor wanted his help and that as a pastor he had failed completely.

No minister can ever live a creative, meaningful life when this feeling becomes predominant. A man who thinks he has no special contribution to his fellow man—that he is considered more as a decoration than an asset to life, more tolerated than needed—will in the long run become depressed, apathetic, dull, and irritable. Or he will simply decide to leave the ministry to enter what he then calls a "real" profession.

But where does that leave Mr. Kern and many people like him? In what kind of condition is a man who does not want to see his own children when he is dying, who curses the doctors who try to give him relief, and who asks for a little corner into which he can crawl away like an animal and perish, not wanting anyone to know or see that he, too, does not have his life in his own hand. Neither medicine nor psychology, neither psychiatry nor social work can ever respond to the final question of why man comes to life, slowly learns to stand on his own feet, attaches himself to someone else, gives life to others, and allows them to continue what he started but will not see fulfilled. A man who has not been able to give meaning to his own life cycle and accept it in its terminable reality cannot die as a *man* but has no other way than the way of animals. It was quite understandable that the head of the section where Mr. Kern stayed asked Michael to go and visit his patient. She knew that Michael could not cure him, but she also realized, perhaps only vaguely, that there is a tremendous difference between dying and slipping away, between giving your life and forsaking it in a hopeless battle, between reaching out to the light that becomes visible in the hour of death and turning away your head and allowing yourself to be drawn into a pit of despair.

Michael might not have been able to make Mr. Kern's death an act of human surrender; life perspectives usually don't change in an hour. But he should at least realize that he was indeed asked to save the life of Mr. Kern—that is, to offer hope, to convert hate into love, to make death an ultimate human gift, and to make it possible for his wife and children to find strength in that same light they saw in the eyes of their husband and father, who was the first to enter it fully.

When a minister discovers that he really can give life to people by enabling them to face their real life-condition without fear, he will at the same time cease looking at himself as a man on the periphery of reality. He is then right in the center. Many doctors realize how dangerous it is to operate on a man who has no will to live, many psychologists are humble enough to confess that they cannot give meaning to life and death—even if they might have many insights into the motivation that makes people hurt and heal each other. Many sociologists know that no structural changes will make sense as long as it remains unclear where such changes will lead. When man no longer sees the meaning of his existence he loses perspective, he grasps what is most satisfying to his immediate needs, escapes in phantasies, sex, and drugs, and finds his life disintegrating to the point of suicide.

Individual pastoral care is in many ways the care most needed and in fact asked for—at least if we can understand the questions. Pastoral training, therefore, perhaps means first of all the education of pastors so that they might hear questions and become aware of the fact that they are needed more than they realize—that thousands of people are constantly asking Alfie's old question: What is it all about anyhow? Why should we eat and drink, work and play, raise money and children, and fight constantly a never-ending sequence of frustrations? Or to say it with the Yoga-vasistha: "What happiness can there be in the world where everyone is born to die?" (cf., W. Allport: *The Individual and his Religion*, Macmillan, 1960, p. 23.)

It is on this level that a minister is called to move. And if he becomes aware of the real questions which are raised right in front of him, he will see that he indeed can touch the heart of life. Then he can cast off his low self-esteem and discover that by affirming the life of his neighbor he is in fact affirming his own ministerial identity.

2. Self-denial

But at the moment when one might start feeling self-confident or proud, a few disturbing words of Christ come to mind: "If anyone wants to be a follower of mine, let him renounce himself—for anyone who loses his life for my sake will find it" (Mt. 16:24–25). Above all, one remembers the almost unbelievable statement of St. Paul: "I live—not with my own life, but with the life of Christ, who lives in me" (Gal. 2:20). Just when the minister might have discovered that he has not only a contribution to give but touches the core of life, just when he is ready to affirm himself, to feel that he is fulfilling his hopes and realizing his deepest aspiration in life, he is faced with the urgent call to deny himself, to consider himself a servant, a useless laborer who is last in line.

Michael put on a white coat so that, just like the medical interns, he might be accepted as one of the team. But the fact is that Michael does not really belong to the hospital, does not have any status or institutional tool. He is not there to cure Mr. Kern. In many ways he is an outsider, who does not know much about illnesses but only about people who happen to be ill. Perhaps his coat is a symbol of his unwillingness to show that he, in fact, has no medical tools or techniques but is allowed to come in from the outside only in order to let Mr. Kern know that although he can do nothing about his cancer, he is nonetheless concerned about the way this patient chooses to live and the way he chooses to die.

Many ministers and priests are extremely concerned to be *in* with the competent people and to have a clear-cut identity. But is it really so important to come to this professional self-fulfillment? The great influence of Freud, Jung, Rogers, and Frankl has raised for many ministers the question: How can I be my real self, personal as well as professional? It seems that the clerical waiting list for sensitivity training has become considerably longer than the one for Trappist guesthouses. But is it our vocation to fulfill our own self to its ultimate degree and to create situations in which we can come to what we consider to be the most meaningful, beautiful, and intensive experience?

Thomas Merton, in one of his later works, wrote:

> It becomes overwhelmingly important for us to become detached from our everyday conception of ourselves as potential subjects for special unique experiences, or as candidates for realisation, attainment and fulfillment.
> (*Zen and the Birds of Appetite*, New Directions, New York, 1960, p. 76.)

If Mr. Kern would have been able to profit from Michael's visit, it certainly would not have been because Michael knew a great deal or had answers to the questions of life, but because he was unarmed and could lose himself for someone else and thereby give him the freedom to talk—not only about his cancer, his problems or present worries, but also about why he lived the way he did and how he is now facing the task of dying.

Nobody can minister to his fellow man when he is unwilling to deny himself in order to create the space where

God can do His work. How can we really be of help to others if we keep concentrating on ourselves? As long as we are trying to keep our mind on things, we are not really concentrated. Falling asleep, in fact, means ceasing to try to do so. Only when a man can forget about himself for a while can he become really interested in another—that is, enter into the center of his concerns.

So self-affirmation and self-denial are both a part of the identity of the minister. Are they contrary to each other? The new understanding of the Zen-Buddhist tradition certainly has made it clear that we feel more at home with the idea of self-fulfillment than with the idea of self-emptying. Dr. H. H. M. Fortmann, the Dutch priest-psychologist, wrote while expecting his own death to come soon:

> . . . the religious problem of the West . . . has to be related to the inflation of the Ego. We have lost the awareness that there is a kind of knowledge, which can only be reached by a reverent process of making loose and empty.
> (*Oosterse Renaissance*, Ambo Bilthoven, 1970, p. 6.)

Since the East-West dialogue has become a part of many people's lives, especially the young, we have become aware of the fact that there are two forms of consciousness: one that says be yourself so you can be creative, and the other that says lose yourself to God can be creative in you. The former stresses individuality, the latter unification.

Pastoral education during recent years has been under the strong influence of Western behavioral sciences. This explains at least part of the emphasis on self and individual creativity. It also makes quite understandable why the search for professional identity in the ministry has received so much attention. But if we read certain signs of the times correctly, it might well be true that the Wise Men from the East again belong to those who truly worship Christ and that the growing interest in the way of Siddhartha, so beautifully described by Hermann Hesse, is a powerful suggestion for the pastor of the future. If the inflation of the pastor's ego prevents his mystical union with God, no Michael can help any Mr. Kern to make death a final act of surrender.

But self-affirmation and self-emptying are not opposites because no man can give away what he does not have. No one can give himself in love when he is not aware of himself. Nobody can come to intimacy without having found his identity. Jesus lived thirty years in a simple family. There He became a man who knew who He was and where He wanted to go. Only then was He ready to empty Himself and give His life for others. That is the way of all ministry. Through long and often painful formation and training, the minister has to find his place in life, to discover his own contribution, and to affirm his own self: not to cling to it and claim it as his own unique property, but to go out, offer his services to others, and empty himself so that God can speak through him and call man to new life.

So the identity of the pastor, as it becomes visible in his pastoral care, is born from the intangible tension between self-affirmation and self-denial, self-fulfillment and self-emptying, self-realization and self-sacrifice. There are periods in life in which the emphasis is more on one than on the other, but in general it seems that as a man becomes more mature he will become less concerned with girding himself and more willing to stretch out his hands and to follow Him who found His life by losing it.

II. SPIRITUALITY AND THE PASTORAL RELATIONSHIP

The growing emphasis on self-denial in the service of the other, besides being crucial for pastoral identity, is also essential to the pastoral relationship. Even if Michael knows quite well what his own role is among the many professionals he is working with, the question nonetheless remains: What is his relationship with Mr. Kern? Mr. Kern did not ask for him, as was quite obvious from the discussion. And why should Michael knock on the door of a stranger? Simply because the head of the section became concerned about his condition? That the doctor visits is understandable since Mr. Kern came to the hospital to be treated by doctors. But in allowing himself to be brought to the hospital Mr. Kern was certainly not expecting to be visited by a complete stranger who was affiliated with a religious organization completely alien to his life. Michael was aware of this. He simply said who he was and where he could be reached. He also explained that three religions were represented in the hospital by a minister, priest, and rabbi, and Mr. Kern could ask for their services whenever he wanted. Mr. Kern, however, did not want any service of this kind, and that would have ended the discussion had Michael not shown a little more interest and asked how ill Mr. Kern had been.

There are two concepts that can help us understand a little better the uniqueness of the pastoral relationship: the concept of the contract and the concept of the covenant.

1. Contract

Many professional relationships between people fail because of an unclear contract. If two people make an appointment with each other, there is a *formal* contract to meet. If one is asking for help and the other giving help, the *informal* contract is that the problem will be the focus of the meeting. But quite often there is a *secret* contract, which does not always become clear. Sometimes a man looks for advice but receives a sermon, or he wants to be listened to but gets a pep talk, or he hopes for information but does not hear more than "hm, hm." Within a pastoral relationship between two people many different expectations, which are often the cause of great frustrations, can exist. The fact that Michael was so deeply frustrated that he felt "kicked in the stomach" was obviously related to his wrong expectation that Mr. Kern would at least be willing to respond to his desire to be of help. And although Mr. Kern's reaction is quite exceptional, there are many pastors whose unhappiness about their individual pastoral care is directly related to the unclarity of the contract. I remember a lady saying to a pastor: "My boy does not want to go to church anymore. What should I do?"

The pastor said: "You do not quite know how you should react to this new situation, do you?"

The lady said: "Yes, that is what I was trying to say, but what I want to know is, what to do."

Here the pastor starts to counsel while the lady wants direct advice. The result, of course, is that the lady goes home unhappy and the pastor feels he did not get anywhere.

People can be helped in many different ways: by support, advice, instruction, a correction, a clarification of feelings, or by just simply listening. But they are never helped if they expect one thing and receive another. And the first responsibility of the pastor is to help his parishioner become aware of the kind of help he really wants and to let him know if he is able to give it to him.

As long as the secret contract remains secret there is an increased chance that unnecessary disappointments will result. The temptation of many pastors is that they become too preoccupied with just one model of personal relationship: pastoral counseling. That model suggests a process in which pastor and parishioner meet in such a way that the parishioner can clarify his feelings and mobilize his energies to find his own way. Often this requires many well-structured meetings, special skills on the part of the pastor, and special attitudes on the part of the parishioner. But this kind of contract is rather rare in a regular parish. More usual are the many short and casual contacts and conversations in the context of which much or little can happen, according to the sensitivity of the pastor.

Some pastors say that they are always busy but have the feeling of never accomplishing anything. This may, of course, be simply the result of poor planning. But when a pastor has really found his own identity he discovers at the same time that it is exactly his task to relate to many people in many different ways. It is, in fact, these alternatives of relating that enable him to exercise a ministry that has many forms and many different possibilities. Within this perspective the desire to have one specialty and to limit oneself to one way of relating is more an escape than a virtue. It is true that this multiformity of the ministry can create great frustration, but this frustration might belong to the essence of the ministry and point to a way of relating that goes beyond the contractual way of the other professions. Let us therefore now look at the concept of the covenant as an important corrective of the contractual view of the pastoral relationship.

2. *Covenant*

The word contract, a predominantly economic term, has become a powerful concept in the field of human relationships. The distinction between the formal, informal, and secret contract has helped very much to clarify many failures in professional relationships between people. It is easy to see, therefore, how it has likewise helped many pastors to better understand the different problems as well as possibilities in their relationships with people.

But just as self-affirmation is not the only aspect of the identity of the minister, so contract is not the last word about the pastoral relationship. Just as Michael went to see Mr. Kern even though he was not invited, so too do many ministers and priests knock on doors, ring bells, and walk into houses where nobody is waiting for them. No doctor would think of going from one house to another to ask if there is anybody ill enough to need his help. No psychologist will call on people to find out if there are emotional problems that will give him a chance to exercise his expertise. But the pastor takes initiatives and can even be considered as an aggressive practitioner who wants "to proclaim the message, welcome or unwelcome, and insist on it" (2 Tim. 4:2).

The fact that the word contract cannot really express the pastoral relationship points to the fact that if a pastor likes to consider his relationship with an individual a professional relationship, his profession is of a different kind from all the other helping professions. And here the biblical term covenant adds a critical note to the contractual view on the pastoral relationship. Yahweh did not establish a contract

with his people, but a covenant. A contract finishes when
one of the partners does not adhere to his promises. Once
a patient no longer pays his doctor, the doctor is free to
prefer another patient instead; so, too, when a man does
not keep his appointments with a psychologist, the psychologist in turn does not feel obligated to visit him and ask him
why he did not come. There is indeed an understandable
cynicism in the joke that calls a psychiatrist a man who is
willing to be your friend for twenty-five dollars an hour.

But Yahweh says: "Does a woman forget her baby at
her breast or fail to cherish the son of her womb? Yes,
even if these forget I will never forget you" (Isaiah 49:15).
And he who understands this covenant responds: "If my
father and mother desert me, Yahweh will care for me
still" (Psalms 27:10). In the final analysis, it is not the
professional contract but the Divine Covenant that is the
basis of a pastoral relationship. In the covenant there is
no condition put on faithfulness. It is the unconditional
commitment to be of service.

This is perhaps the greatest challenge to everyone who
wants to make God's covenant visible in this world: for
who does not expect a return for his good services? Perhaps
we do not ask for money after a pastoral conversation, perhaps we do not even expect a small gift at Christmas or
a word of thanks, but can we really detach ourselves from
our subtle condition of change? A very good friend of mine,
a priest who decided to become a bartender in Amsterdam,
said one day: "I don't want to be called pastor because
I have seen too many so-called pastors who are spiritual
prostitutes selling their love under the condition of change.
If my relationship with a man is affected by the subtle
pressure that he should stop drinking so much, get away

from drugs, be less promiscuous, cut his long hair, go to court, to church, or the city hall, I am still not really with him but with my own preoccupations, value systems and expectations, and have made of myself a prostitute and degraded my fellow man by making him a victim of my spiritual manipulations." Many ministers complain that nobody says thanks to them, that hours spent with people don't bring about any change in them, that after many years of teaching, preaching, counseling, organizing, and celebrating people are still apathetic, the church still authoritarian, and the society still corrupt. But if our gratification has to come from visible change, we have made God into a businessman and ourselves into sales managers.

Michael received no thanks for his honest desire to be of help, but even after Mr. Kern's remark, "I do not care to talk," he said, "still I would like to drop in from time to time if for no more than to say Hello, just to see how things are with you." That reaction does not make sense to a man who looks for gratification, though we can perhaps nonetheless discover in the awkward and unhandy approach of Michael something of God's faithfulness, which by its incomprehensibility can evoke irritation as well as sympathy.

So we have seen that the pastoral relationship can never completely be understood within the logic of a professional contract. Every man asks for thanks, hopes for success, and expects change to come about—the minister as much as anyone else. But God did not offer us a contract but a covenant, and challenges those who want to make His covenant visible in this world never to make human success a criterion of their love for man.

III.   SPIRITUALITY AND THE PASTORAL APPROACH

When the identity of the minister is found in the creative tension between self-affirmation and self-denial and when the nature of the pastoral relationship carries the signs of a professional contract but is ultimately based on the covenant of God with His people, we are left with the question of the pastoral approach. Can anything be said about how a minister or priest should specifically behave when he finds himself in a one-to-one relationship with someone in need of help?

What should Michael have done when he entered Mr. Kern's room? Was it wrong to start talking about the variety of services the hospital had to offer? Should he have acted differently, said something else, or absolutely nothing? Should he have asked how Mr. Kern was doing after he had just heard that Mr. Kern was not at all in the mood to talk? These were probably Michael's main problems when he came to his supervisor. He might have said: "Okay, I did a miserable job. I even feel guilty about it, but—tell me what should I have done or said?"

Many ministers and priests today take special training exactly because of their need to be more skillful in their individual pastoral relationships. The increasing number of pastoral training centers is witness to the great desire to find an answer to the "how to do it" question. How to have a good conversation with students? How to help a man in a crisis situation? How to relate to the hippie or the young radical? How to have a meaningful contact with the confused teen-ager or the rebellious young adult? How to help an embittered dying patient? How to do this and how to do that? Sometimes I have the strange feeling that we are still too preoccupied with the old doctor's problem of how to get the child to swallow the bitter pill. Sweetening the pill, music in the background, or a distracting puppet show? But the pill has to be swallowed. Quite often pastors look to the masters of the behavioral sciences to give them answers for their urgent questions. And many psychologists, sociologists, counselors, and sensitivity trainers become rich today by teaching their ways to eager ministers who admire their skills and hope to find in them a solution for their deep-seated feelings of inadequacy.

I do not want to underestimate the tremendous importance of the great help the social sciences can offer to the pastor. One of the main reasons for great hope in the field of pastoral care is precisely the still developing dialogue between pastors, sociologists, social workers, psychologists, and psychiatrists. But I also feel that there is a unique dimension to pastoral care that goes beyond the expertise of the behavioral sciences and even beyond professionalism. It is to that dimension that I would like to pay special attention here. I would like to do this by focussing on one specific aspect of many new forms of pastoral training: the writing of the pastoral report.

One of the most important things pastors learn in their training is to write down their experiences. Charles Hall, executive secretary of the Clinical Pastoral Education movement, once said: "What is worth saying is worth writing." If Michael had not written down his painful pastoral visit, he could not have learned much from his experience. But what was there to be learned? I would like to discuss this by using two terms: Role Definition and Contemplation.

1. Role definition

It is no secret that ministers are not accustomed to writing. A good number, of course, boast: "Oh, I could write a book about things that happen in this parish." But very few do. The doctor writes his medical report, the psychologist his test report, the social worker his case report. But most pastors do not have any document available to help them define their own role. Russel Dicks, one of the pioneers of the clinical training movement, says: "We believe that until the minister develops a method of keeping records of his own with individuals, he has no right to claim a place for himself among the skilled workers in the field of human personality." (*The Art of Ministering to the Sick,* Macmillan, New York, 1936, p. 256.)

By studying the written reports of his pastoral work with individuals, the minister is able to clarify his own experience. He also has a concrete way of identifying exactly what happened in his pastoral work and a unique chance to think realistically about alternative ways of pastoral behavior. In this way he is able to define what took place and what has to be done. When Michael looked over the report of his visit to Mr. Kern, he realized that his nervousness had made him cling to concrete information and behave more like an officer of a tourist bureau than a pastor. He also became aware that he could have prevented much pain if before the visit he had asked the doctor or nurse something about Mr. Kern—his religion and his physical and psychological condition. He started wondering whether his white coat, which of course made him look like a doctor, had not created most of the hostility. He was likewise able to think about different ways of relating to an extremely hostile and bitter man, who was unable to face his situation and unable to show his need for human help. So Michael learned from his experience. But experience is a very ambivalent word. Many priests, who use their years of experience as an argument for their competence, tend to forget that only a few people learn from experience. One carefully reported and critically evaluated event can often teach a man more than many years filled with experiences empty of understanding. When a man, however, can define where he stands he can also draw a map of where he wants to go. Every professional is responsible for his own definition. When a priest cannot define his role carefully, he will never be able to make it clear to anyone else. Michael started to define his role when he wrote down his experiences. Perhaps his next visit was a little less frustrating because of it.

But if we look upon role definition as the last word in individual pastoral care, then we miss the core of the ministry, which is not skillful practice but reverent contemplation. It would be well, therefore, to finally examine the meaning of contemplation.

2. *Contemplation*

The great concern of many supervisors such as Russel Dicks has been to help ministers learn the best response to a given stimulus. Michael's responses to Mr. Kern's stimuli certainly could have been a lot better. Many alternative responses are imaginable. And although it would be naïve to say that a minister should stay away from all special skills, tools, and techniques in human relationships—we might even wish he had a few more!—skillful responses certainly do not constitute the core of the ministry. He who writes down his experiences does not only have a chance to define the event and the best response to it, but also has an invaluable source of theological contemplation. When Anton Boisen, the father of the clinical training movement, asked his students to write down their experiences, he did not think first of all about the "how to do it well" question, but, rather, about the question, "What can I learn from this person whom I meet as a pastor." For him the most forgotten source of theology was what he called "the living human document." In *The Exploration of the Inner World* he writes:

> Just as no historian worthy of the name is content to accept on authority the simplified statement of some other historian regarding the problem under investigation, so I have sought to begin not with the ready made formulations contained in books, but with living human documents and with actual social conditions in all their complexities.
>
> (Harper Torchbooks, New York, p. 135.)

For a man of faith no meeting is accidental. Mr. Kern and Michael met. And even though Michael was in no way able to help him as he thought he could, perhaps Mr. Kern told Michael something he should never forget: A man can become so hard, so bitter, and so disappointed in life that the only wish he has left is to be allowed to crawl into a corner and die like an animal. Mr. Kern shows in a most naked and terrifying way the condition in which a man can find himself when he loses faith in the possibility of love.

Michael might have read Kierkegaard, Sartre, Camus, Kafka, and many others who write about anxiety and guilt, loneliness and alienation, sin, and death. But now he stands face to face with a man who says: "You will do me a favor if you leave—and do not return." Michael might have said: "Oh, just another stubborn, proud fellow who wants to be left alone"—but then he would not be really contemplating the condition of man as it becomes visible in Mr. Kern's despair.

Mr. Kern does much more than refuse to talk. He is a living, human document which can give rise to the most fundamental questions of theology: questions of sin and salvation, guilt and forgiveness, isolation and reconciliation, and, finally, of life and death. In his case, however, these questions become more than theoretical—they have immediate implications for the understanding of everyone relating to him: the doctors, whom he could no longer face; his children, whom he refused to see while dying; his wife, who will live on with a memory of an embittered husband; and Michael, who wanted to help him die but could not.

Pastoral care means much more than pastoral worries. It means a careful and critical contemplation of the condition of man. Through this contemplation the pastor can take away the veil and make visible to himself and to others the fact that good and evil are not just words but visible realities in the life of every man. In this sense, every pastoral contact is a challenge to understand in a new way God's work with man and to distinguish with a growing sensitivity the light and the darkness in the human heart.

In this way, contemplation is not just an important aspect of the life of the priest or an indispensable condition for a fruitful ministry. Ministry *is* contemplation. It is the ongoing unveiling of reality and the revelation of God's light as well as man's darkness. In this perspective, individual pastoral care can never be limited to the application of any skill or technique since ultimately it is the continuing search for God in the life of the people we want to serve. The paradox of the ministry indeed is that we will find the God we want to give in the lives of the people to whom we want to give Him.

And so we have seen that if the pastoral approach does not go beyond the level of skills and techniques, the minister is tempted to become a manipulator of people. Only when he learns to see his pastoral relationships as a vital source of theological contemplation can he himself also be ministered to by those whom he cares for.

CONCLUSION

The main purpose of this chapter has been to show the implications of individual pastoral care for the personal life of the minister himself. I hope that the central movement from professionalism to spirituality has been clear. In the search for his professional identity, the minister moves from self-affirmation to self-denial; in the establishment of a professional relationship, he moves from contract to covenant; and in his professional approach to the individual needs of his fellow man, he moves from role-definition to contemplation.

If a minister wants to be of real help in his contact with people, he has to be a professional with special information, special training, and special skills. But if he wants to break through the chains of our manipulative world, he has to move beyond professionalism, and through self-denial and contemplation, become a faithful witness of God's covenant.

Only Jesus can be called pastor in this sense. He cared for many people in their most individual needs. He cared for the woman at the well, for Mary Magdalene, for Nicodemus, and for the men traveling to Emmaus who felt their hearts burn when He talked with them. Jesus was certainly skillful in His relationships with people and was not afraid to use His insights into the stirrings of the human heart. But when asked about the source of his knowledge, He said:

> My teaching is not from myself; it comes from the One who sent me. When a man's doctrine is his own, he is hoping to get honour for himself; but when he is working for the honor of one who sent him, then he is sincere and by no means an imposter.
>
> (John 7:16–18)

The minister who cares for people is called to be skillful but not a handyman, knowledgeable but not an imposter, a professional but not a manipulator. When he is able to deny himself, to be faithful and to understand the meaning of human suffering, then the man who is cared for will discover that through the hands of those who want to be of help God shows his tender love for him.

CHAPTER IV

BEYOND THE MANIPULATION OF STRUCTURES

ORGANIZING

INTRODUCTION

When we want to examine the relationship between organizing and spirituality, we can perhaps start nowhere better than with the many painful questions asked by ministers and priests who have become aware of their vocation to be agents of change.

After many hours, days, and years of teaching, preaching, and individual pastoral care, most ministers suddenly stop and ask themselves:

> Why do I spend so much time in preaching the Word of God while those I really would like to reach are never in my church? Why do I teach children and adults to prepare them for a society that for many does not offer even the possibility of living the life I am trying to advocate? Why do I call people together to celebrate their unity while they are not able to live together in peace but are torn apart by hate, competition, and segregation?

> Why do I spend so many hours talking about the individual pains of people, while I leave the society that creates these pains unchanged?

There is a growing frustration in the life of many ministers and priests because of the awareness that their everyday work does not really touch the structures of life. They feel like people who help the wounded but are unable to stop the war. Their words in the pulpit, the classroom, and the rectory may be a support to many people and give them the courage to face their lives again, but what about the sick society itself suffering from war, pollution, poverty, crimes, and violence? When there is something basically wrong with the world in which we live, what help are all our words?

Is it our task to help people adapt to a society that is not worth adapting to? What does it mean to talk to a woman who does not have enough bread for her children? No counseling skill will take away her hunger. What does it mean to preach love and understanding in a community where people have no decent houses to live in, no jobs to earn a living, where children have no space to play, and where most people have lost faith in the words of those who announce a better world to come?

More and more priests are haunted by these questions and wonder if the church has not in fact moved away to the periphery of life and, although still caring for people, has failed to change the structures of society itself in order to make a real Christian life possible.

Over the last years this awareness has grown and many ministers and priests are wondering if it is really possible to become agents of social change, to extend their pastoral care not only to individuals but to social structures as well. New training centers have developed, such as the Ecumenical Institute and the Urban Training Center in Chicago. In such places the first question is not: How can I help this man who has a problem, but: How can I help this society change so that fewer people have problems? The focus is not so much on the pastoral relationship and the pastoral approach, but on the careful analysis of the social situation, the definition of the specific issue at hand, the inventory of the sources of the community, and the development of a careful strategy to bring about social change.

But what is the task of the minister and priest in the complex field of community organization? When that term suggests that it is the task of a minister to take all the responsibility for many specific projects into his own hands, I certainly would say No, but when it indicates the vocation to make people aware of their hidden potentialities, to unify the many different self-interests into a common concern, to remove the paralyzing influence of fatalism, and to offer a vision that makes people see their social responsibility and strive beyond the many concrete actions to a Christian community in faith, then he might very well consider himself an organizer in a very unique way. He can awaken the dormant powers in his milieu. He can break through the chains of pessimism and collective depression and make his people aware that things do not necessarily have to be the way they are. He can prevent people from falling back in apathy after unexpected disappointments and from using destructive escapisms instead of constructive action. He can help create a mentality of hope and confidence, which makes a community flexible and adaptable to new situations and always alert for new possibilities and new perspectives.

In this sense, a minister and priest can be an agent of social change without having to be trapped in the pitfalls of a manipulative world. But this requires a spirituality, a way of living that allows man to be very much involved in this world precisely because he is free toward it and does not cling to it with a destructive possessiveness. To describe this spirituality we first have to identify the different dangers to which man is exposed in his social activities. Therefore, I will divide this chapter in two parts: 1) the pitfalls of the organizer and 2) the Christian agent of social change.

I. THE PITFALLS OF THE ORGANIZER

When we ask people about the condition of our world today we quickly become aware that many of them have come to the conclusion that our society is so completely rotten and its structures so totally a failure that the only solution to the problem is a total structural and social change. They are willing to fight for it and do anything possible to make this new society come about. They have become aware that the slogan "Change the world by beginning with yourself" does not work, and that, rather, if man truly wants to change, then the world in which he lives has to change first. They feel that changing people without changing the structures is a waste of time and that real change has to come from the outside, even if violence, cruelty, and execution have to be used to bring it about. This is the attitude of the commissar of the Russian Revolution as described by Arthur Koestler (*The Yogi and the Commissar*, Collier Books, New York). This is also the attitude of those many revolutionaries today who burn banks, destroy property, create street fights, and do everything possible to upset the existing order in the conviction that the new world will be born out of the ashes of the old. There are probably very few ministers and priests who share this conviction in all its consequences. However, many of them, who have become deeply aware of the overwhelming problems of our society, might nonetheless be inclined to suggest tactics and strategies that are still based on the supposition that man will only change if the structures change first.

It seems to me there are three pitfalls, three dangers, that
threaten this type of social activism: concretism, power, and
pride.

1. The danger of concretism

The danger of concretism is the inclination to make very concrete and specific results the main motivation for continuing
social action. Many times it seems that much of the suffering
and frustration of people working in ghettos, slums, or under-
developed areas is the result of the fact that the changes
they hoped to accomplish did not come about. They start
their work with great enthusiasm and generous willingness
to be of help, but after a few years, when they see that
not much has changed and that the situation is still essentially the same as when they started, they leave disappointed
and sometimes bitter, hurt by a loss of self-esteem and the
feeling of failure and worthlessness. Not a few Peace Corps
men, Vista workers, and Papal Volunteers can witness to
this experience.

Quite often the reason for this attitude is that they enter
their work with preconceived ideas about how things should
be, as if they were saying: *"This* is what these people need"
—better houses, better education, better recreation facilities,
sewer systems, labor unions, cooperatives, etc. But these very
specific aims might well ruin their effectiveness, make them
blind to what people really need, and deaf to what they say.
So, often, totally in contrast with their desire, they create
hostility in the people they want to help.

I remember once working in a very poor Dutch neighborhood. I visited a family with ten children, who were
walking around in rags during the day and sleeping together

in three large old beds at night. So I felt the help they needed was obvious. I ordered some clothes and bought a few more beds. But later, when I entered the house unexpectedly, there was a big party going on with beer and cakes. My good friends had sold the beds and most of the clothes in order to invite their friends and neighbors in to celebrate the birthday of their eldest son. Actually, they had enough clothes—though they didn't know how to repair them—and sleeping in a separate bed seemed quite lonely for most of the children.

It is quite obvious that my help was more an expression of what I thought a good life ought to be rather than what they thought about it. This same kind of mistake is made in many situations. New houses, for example, are given to people without realizing that living in them might not be nearly as important as living close to one's friends.

A good number of population programs have totally failed because well-meaning helpers were handing out their new technological inventions, pills, I.U.Ds, and other contraceptives without carefully asking themselves how people feel about having large families, what it means to a man and his wife to have none or only a few children, and how other populations judge the values of life. Quite often sex education has been considered as a solution to problems without a careful study of the motivation of people's sexual behavior, and new expensive programs have been endorsed as if all people think, feel, and act alike. In short, our own preconceived concretionary views have caused more hindrance than assistance in our attempts to improve our world and help our fellow man.

2. *The danger of power*

People who organize are in constant danger of creating small kingdoms for themselves. It is extremely difficult to take initiatives and develop new plans without claiming it as something that is yours. Just as many parents find it hard to let their children choose their own life-styles, so too do many "organizing priests" want to keep running the show and telling people what to do.

One way of exercising power over people is to become subject to what Dr. John Santos, head of the psychology department at the University of Notre Dame, calls the Education-Enlightenment hypothesis—that is, the hypothesis that makes us think that if we tell people what makes good sense to us, it will automatically make good sense to them as well. Many social reformers still think that when you give people the right information and the right instructions they will become so enlightened they will do exactly what you have in mind. But people do not always feel that those things you consider to be good for them necessarily are so. Many well-intentioned projects written up by many well-educated people have been ignored and even ridiculed by those who have other values and perspectives. While you think a hundred-dollar bill is worth much, someone else might just light his cigarette with it. Education itself can become a form of power when we think that we are helping people by presenting them with our value system as the ideal way of life. The black-power movement was, in part, a reaction against the education-enlightenment hypothesis that made us think that the black man would be much happier if he were allowed to share the white man's way of life. But, in fact, this only means that education has become propaganda and that offering help has become part of the power game.

The most subtle desire for power, and the most difficult to overcome is the desire for thanks. As long as people keep thanking us for what we have done for them, they are, in effect, admitting that they were at least for some time dependent on us. And it is perhaps exactly for this reason that we find in areas where people are living in very poor conditions a certain resistance against explicit thankfulness. Nobody likes to be considered in need of help or as not being able to take care of himself—facts which an expression of thanks often explicitly asserts. It should therefore come as no surprise that men and women who have spent many days helping others seldom hear a word of thanks. It would only be, in such cases, a reminder of dependency and a threat to self-respect. Not only individuals but even whole countries have thus refused gifts of money and badly needed medicine because they preferred to die with what self-respect they had rather than to live with the feeling that others have to keep them on their feet.

But for the man who is aware of the need of people and wants to do something about it, it is difficult to live without at least a small kingdom of thankful people who are willing to say that without him they would not be who they are now or do what they do now.

3. *The danger of pride*

Finally, there is the great temptation of pride. Everyone who wants to change society is in danger of putting himself above it and being more conscious of the weaknesses of others than of the weakness in his own soul. The reformer, who is convinced that things have to become different, is out to convert the world but is tempted at the same time to think that he himself does not need conversion. Instead of seeing himself as a full member of that same society which needs reform, he might approach it with the fantasy of a redeemer who himself is untouchable and is always right and just.

He might see the cruel segregation between races but be blind to the fact that what he sees dramatically happening on the world scene is also happening in himself when he condemns certain people as being stupid, others as being narrow-minded, and still others as being conceited. He might be very critical of capitalism and the waste of money but not see that his own style of life would be impossible without the capitalistic society he condemns. He might feel that many people should have a better life and more human respect but at the same time be unable to listen to people, accept their criticism and believe that he can learn from them. He might always be busy going from one meeting to another and forget that he himself tends to lose contact with the sources of his own existence and become deaf to the voice that calls from within. He might even be afraid to be alone and face the fact that he himself is in just as much need of change as the world he wants to convert.

The three dangers of every man who is concerned about social change are, therefore, concretism, power, and pride. When Jesus had become aware of His vocation to criticize the society in which He lived, to question its basic supposition, and to work for the Kingdom to come, He knew that He too could have become an organizer in the long row of those who had already called themselves Messiahs. And indeed He was tempted to bring about immediate results and change the stones into bread, to take the power and the glory of all the kingdoms of the world, and to prove His invulnerability by throwing Himself down from the parapet of the temple and allowing the angels to guard Him.

But only through overcoming these temptations could He become a revolutionary man who was able to break through the narrowing chains of His world and surpass all political ambitions in order to make visible the new Kingdom to come. In this sense, Herbert McCabe is right when he says:

The likeliest model for the Christian minister—is the revolutionary leader: indeed, the priest should be a

revolutionary leader, but one who goes in and through
what in today's terms is called a political revolution to
a depth which today we call metaphysical or spiritual.
This interpretation of the revolution in its ultimate
depths *is* the proclamation of the gospel—

(*Priesthood and Revolution,* Commonweal,
September 20, 1968, p. 626.)

We are now ready to ask ourselves what the main traits
are of the man who wants to be a Christian agent of social
change.

II. THE CHRISTIAN AGENT

Every man who has become aware of the illnesses of the
society in which he lives and feels a growing need to work
for social change is faced with the temptations of concretism, power, and pride. And many have become so deeply
impressed by these temptations that they do not see how to
avoid them. It almost seems that being an agent for social
change and a Christian becomes a contradiction. Many ask
themselves: How can I work for a better world without
developing hate against those who contradict me, without
being tempted to gossip, conspiracy, and hatred? How can I
work for the deprived black man without sharing his hostile
feelings for the white? How can I help the poor without
hating those whom I see as their exploiters? How can I criticize the Establishment without being conceited, self-
righteous, and close-minded? In short, how can I actively
work for a better world and not harm the Christian values
that tell me to love my enemies as well as my friends?

Many people who become hurt in this struggle for social
reform have indeed become so overwhelmed by this problem
that in order to avoid becoming like the commissar who

was willing to sacrifice the individual to change the structure, they choose what is in effect the opposite way: the way of the Yogi. It is not difficult to understand why many people, tired by social action and disappointed with its results, have chosen the inward way. All over the country we see new centers of meditation and concentration in which people try to come to terms with this chaotic world by changing the world from within and making themselves internally free. Quite often they have turned to the East to find a new way. Many have become so deeply convinced that all the conflicts of the world find their origins in the human heart and that their internal life is just a miniature of the cruel battlefields of the large society, that for them the only real place to start changing the world is to start in the center of their own inner life.

Arthur Koestler writes: "The Yogi believes that nothing can be changed by external organisation, but everything by the individual attempt from within, and that everyone who thinks otherwise escapes the real problem." (*The Yogi and the Commissar.*

It might be worthwhile to ask if the growing interest in the Pentecostal movement within the Catholic Church is not in some way an expression of this same attitude. By concentration on inner conversion and the eradication of evil from the human heart, by stressing personal love and the creation of small communities of prayer, many deeply committed Pentecostals are basically saying that the only way to change our destructive world is to start with a change in one's own heart. It is not surprising, therefore, to find that the Pentecostal, like the Yogi, has often been accused of being aloof and indifferent to the great social problems of war, poverty, pollution, segregation, social injustice, and crime, and of having escaped into a personal garden where he can concentrate on his own soul, experience the stirrings of the Spirit, and make his own conversion the criterion for the solutions of the problems of this world.

But neither the commissar nor the Yogi, neither the radical Christian reformer nor the Pentecostal are able to solve the problems of our society. The great task of the minister, rather, is to live and to help live in the tension between both and search for a synthesis. The Christian agent of social change is called upon to be a social reformer and a man who does not lose his own soul, a man of action and a man of prayer at the same time. He is called upon to be concerned with the large issues of our time without losing sight of the children, the poor, the sick, and the old, who ask for our personal care and attention. In a Christian perspective, this careful balance becomes a possibility. Living in this perspective and opening it for the members of his community, the minister becomes a true agent of social change. And we can even say that insofar as a Christian makes this perspective visible, he in fact becomes a minister to men. I would therefore like now to describe this perspective as a perspective of hope, of creative receptivity, and of shared responsibility.

1. *The perspective of hope*

Gabriel Marcel has made it clear that what many people call hope is in fact a form of wish-fulfillment thinking. The life of any man is filled with wishes. A child wishes for a bicycle, a boy wishes for a football, a student wishes for a good grade, a man wishes for a car, a house, a job. A sick man wishes to be cured; a poor man, to become rich; a prisoner, to become free. This wish-fulfillment thinking is like waiting for a Santa Claus whose task it is to satisfy very specific needs and desires, if possible, immediately. When the life of a man is filled with this type of specific concrete wish, however, he is in constant danger of becoming disappointed, bitter, angry, or indifferent since more often than not his wishes don't come true, and he comes to feel that somewhere and somehow he has been betrayed.

I have the feeling that many ministers and priests working for social change are often the victims of this wish-fulfillment thinking. They work for better housing, better schools, or a better neighborhood. They have very concrete goals in mind and very specific ways to realize them. But although the goals are important and the means reasonable, they tend, nonetheless, to make the fulfillment of their wishes the criterion for their own self-esteem. Basically, they are still men of little faith, who are more concerned with the gift they want than the giver from whom they want it.

Only through hope is a man able to overcome this concretionary attitude, for hope is not directed to the gift but to Him who is the giver of all good. We wish *that*, but we hope *in*.* Essential to hope, therefore, is that man does not ask for guarantees, does not put conditions to his actions, does not ask for insurance, but expects everything from the other without putting any limit on his trust. Perhaps the best example of a hopeful attitude is still that of the attitude of a child towards his mother. He is constantly asking for very concrete things, but his love for his mother does not depend upon the fulfillment of these wishes. The child knows that the mother wants only the good for him— although he might cry or even be very angry at times, he keeps living in the conviction that his mother wants only what is good for him.

* See Paul Pruyser, *A Dynamic Psychology of Religion* (Harper & Row, 1968), pp. 166–70.

He who works for social change usually has very specific things in mind, as he must, but he can only remain a man of faith when he views every result he has achieved as a gift to him which he is asked to accept in freedom. Nobody can force the soul of a community. The only possibility open is to create conditions in which the community can freely develop and discover the ways that lead to redemption.

A man of hope can give all his energy, time, and abilities to the people he works for, but when he attaches himself to any specific result he might lose sight of his ultimate objective. Through his attitude of hope, the agent of social change does not fall into the temptation of concretism. He does not worry about the results of his work because he believes that God will fulfill his promises and that it is only a temptation to desire to know exactly how this will happen. In the same way, a man and a woman who promise faithfulness to each other do not want to know how things will look twenty years later. Only when they leave their future open can they prevent disappointments and receive the results of their mutual relationship as a gift.

When a Christian can offer this perspective of hope he makes man free to look beyond the immediate needs of the community and understand his activities in a larger perspective. Perhaps there is no better example of this type of leadership than the leadership given by Martin Luther King. He stimulated his people to work for very concrete rights, an equal place on the bus and in the restaurant and an equal right to vote, but at the same time he never made this an ultimate value but always looked beyond the results of his actions to the larger issue involved: the total freedom of the human person. Therefore, he could say that not only the black man was unfree, but the white, who suppressed him, as well. Therefore, he could prevent people from using violence when a desired goal was not accomplished. Therefore, he could give himself totally for the cause of civil rights even while knowing that he would not see the results. Therefore, he was not afraid of death. In the midst of all activities, he kept reminding his people that although few wishes were fulfilled and few changes brought about, there was no reason for despair. He kept reminding his followers that they were on the road to the promised land and that they had to cross the desert first to reach the place where God would make His people free. Martin Luther King was able to exercise such a powerful spiritual leadership because, although he asked for freedom NOW, he had learned to be patient and wait until God's will fulfilled His promises.

2. *The perspective of a creative receptivity*

By developing in himself and others the willingness to receive, the minister can prevent man from falling into the temptation of power. He who wants to bring about change has first of all to learn to be changed by those whom he wants to help. This, of course, is exceptionally difficult for those who are undergoing their first exposure to an area of distress. They see poor houses, hungry people, dirty streets, they hear people cry in pain without medical care, they smell unwashed bodies, and in general are overwhelmed by the misery which is all around them. But no man will be able to really give if he has not discovered that what he gives is only a small thing compared to what he has received. When Jesus says: "happy the poor, the hungry, and the weeping" (Lk. 6:21), we have to be able to *see* that happiness. When Jesus says: "What you did to the least of my brothers, you did to me" (Mt. 25:40), he is addressing to us a direct invitation not only to help but also to discover the beauty of God in those who are to be helped. As long as a man sees only distasteful poverty, he is not really entitled to give. When, however, we find people who have truly devoted themselves to work in the slums and the ghettos and who feel that their vocation is to be of service there, we find that they have discovered that in the smiles of the children, the hospitality of the people, the expressions they use, the stories they tell, the wisdom they show, the goods they share, there is hidden so much richness and beauty, so much affection and human warmth, that the work they are doing is only a small return for what they have already received. In this respect we can better understand those many missionaries who, after living for years in the poorest circumstances, nonetheless became homesick for their missions as soon as they returned to their affluent country. It was not because they wanted to suffer more, but because they had found a beauty in their people which they missed in their home community.

There are many countries, cities, and neighborhoods that need help, and it is sad to see that we still believe that the best way to motivate others to offer their assistance is to show through books and photographs how humanely these people have to live. This certainly creates enough guilt feelings to make people open their wallets and give some money, thereby soothing their consciences for a while. But this is not a Christian response. That the exposure of misery can evoke not only pity but also aggression has become quite clear in concentration camps, in films about dying children in Biafra, and in the endless exposure of emaciated bodies by TV, radio, and newspaper. As long as we want to change the condition of other people because we feel guilty about our wealth, we are still playing the power game and waiting for thanks. But when we start discovering that in many ways we are the poor and those who need our help are the wealthy, who have a lot to give, no true social agent gives in to the temptation of power since he has discovered that his task is not a heavy burden or a brave sacrifice but an opportunity to see more and more of the face of Him whom he wants to meet. I wish that more books were written about the so-called "poor" countries and "poor" cities, not only to show how poor they are and how much help they need, but also to show the beauty of their lives, their sayings, their customs, their way of life. Perhaps a new form of Christian "tourism" could then develop in which those who travel can enrich their lives with the wisdom, knowledge, and experience of their hosts.

3. The perspective of shared responsibility

When we think about leaders we still tend to think of individuals with special talents. And indeed, when we think of Pope John, John F. Kennedy, Martin Luther King, and Dag Hammarskjold, we easily realize that they were agents of social change with exceptional influence on the lives of many people—even on the course of history. But it would be a mistake to keep waiting for people like them to do the great things. Not too long ago I talked with a black sociologist and asked him about the leadership in the black community. He said: "Perhaps we needed men like King, but now more than ever it is important to look not so much for individuals as for communities which are able to bring about change."

If Christian laymen, ministers, and priests really want to be agents of social change, the first thing they have to learn is how to share leadership. We are used to saying to people that they have responsibilities. To say that they also have the authority which goes with it, however, is something else. It is amazing to find that most priests are still working very much on their own and have not yet found the creative ways to mobilize the potential leadership in their parishes and share their responsibilities with others.

First of all, there is the fact that there are still only a few parishes where the priests really know what the others are doing. While no hospital or school can function without regular staff conferences, it is still a great exception to see parishes where the common concerns are regularly discussed, analyzed, and evaluated and where there is any kind of strategy or long-range planning. Secondly, the laymen are rarely, if at all, invited to participate in the pastoral work. At the same time, when a priest is busy complaining that he is overworked with visiting the sick and the old, directing meetings, taking care of the finances and other odds and ends, he is also failing to realize that real leadership means a delegation of tasks. Thirdly, no parish in any city can be considered as its own little kingdom. When pastors and laymen from different parishes can come together regularly, discuss their common problems, utilize each other's talents, exchange ideas, unite projects, work out common plans in terms of teaching, preaching, pastoral care, and financing; when they can critically evaluate the main problems of their city, raise their voices together when needed, and let the people know that the Christian community is deeply concerned about the crucial issues of the day, then the church cannot be ignored, and although a great deal of irritation and even open hostility might be the result, we could at least then be certain that God's Word is again a word that must be taken seriously.

The problem of pride, of course, still remains. The remark "mind your own business" can also be heard in the mouths of many Christians. It is not easy to say that you cannot do something yourself, that you are in need of constant criticism, that you are willing to be reminded that the problems of the society are also part of your problems. But whenever pastoral workers, ministers, priests, and laymen come to-gether in a spirit of charity and humility, new things will start happening.

These pastoral staff meetings can, of course, easily be misunderstood as meetings in the spirit of the commissar with the primary purpose of working out strategies and planning careful attacks on social problems. But it does not have to be that way. In the middle of a *poblacion* in Santiago, where poverty, hunger, and misery are all around, priests and sisters nonetheless come together for many hours a week, not primarily to formulate a plan of action, but to share each other's experiences, to carefully contemplate the reality in which they live, to make each other see why people do what they do and say what they say, and to celebrate the Eucharist together as a thanksgiving for being allowed to be of service to the people. Outsiders might of course say: "Why don't you go to work, why do you spend so much time together when there are still so many people who do not have enough to eat and to drink?" But these men and women know that to be real agents of change they have to be contemplatives at heart, able to hear the voice of God in the middle of the crying children, and see His face behind the dirty curtain of misery.

We have now seen how the perspective of hope prevents man from being tempted to look for immediate results, how it can help him avoid the pitfalls of power through the perspective of receptivity, and how it can temper individual pride by a shared responsibility which allows mutual criti-cism as well as mutual support.

Through living in these perspectives, the minister can become a catalyst; that is, a man who can uncover the hidden potentials of his community and channel them into creative social action.

CONCLUSION

The general question of this chapter was: What is the relationship between spirituality and organization? This question led us to the more specific problem: How can the minister be a real agent of change? We discussed the attitude of the commissar, who wants to change the structures first—even if he has to use power and sacrifice people to come to the concrete results he thinks are indispensable for the new world to come. We also discussed the attitude of the inward man, who feels that only by changing the hearts of the individual can we change the structures of our society. But just as the social activist is in danger of forgetting that the pains of our society are also to be found in the heart of the reformer, so too does the inward man easily overlook the colossal problems of our society that go far beyond the personal insights of any individual man. The Christian, layman, priest, or minister who wants to be an agent of social change is constantly challenged to look for the creative synthesis between the social activist and the inward man. To avoid concretism, power, and pride, he has to live in the perspectives of hope, receptivity, and shared responsibility—all of which means that he must be a contemplative man. Christian life is not a life divided between times for action and times for contemplation. No. Real social action is a way of contemplation, and real contemplation is the core of social action. In the final analysis, action and contemplation are two sides of the same reality which makes a man an agent of change. Only the synthesis between the commissar and the Yogi makes it possible, therefore, to be a real agent of social change and to avoid the traps of manipulation. Only this synthesis allows us to look beyond all political, social, and economic developments in order to keep us forever awake and always waiting for a new world to come. For a Christian is only a Christian when he unceasingly asks critical questions of the society in which he lives and continuously stresses the necessity for conversion, not only of the individual but also of the world. A Christian is only a Christian when he refuses to allow himself or anyone else to settle into a comfortable rest. He remains dissatisfied with the *status quo*. And he believes that he has an essential role to play in the realization of the new world to come—even if he cannot say how that world will come about. A Christian is only a Christian when he keeps saying to everyone he meets that the good news of the Kingdom has to be proclaimed to the whole world and witnessed to all nations (Mt. 24:13). As long as a Christian lives he keeps searching for a new order without divisions between people, for a new structure that allows every man to shake hands with every other man, and a new life in which there will be lasting unity and peace. He will not allow his neighbor to stop moving, to lose courage, or to escape into small everyday pleasures to which he can cling. He is irritated by satisfaction and self-content in himself as well as in others since he knows, with an unshakable certainty, that something great is coming of which he has already seen the first rays of light. He believes that this world not only passes but has to pass in order to let the new world be born. He believes that there will never be a moment in this life in which one can rest in the supposition that there is nothing left to do. But he will not despair when he does not see the result he wanted to see. For in the midst of all his work he keeps hearing the words of the One sitting on the throne: "I am making the whole of creation new" (Rev. 21:5).

CHAPTER V

BEYOND THE PROTECTIVE RITUAL

CELEBRATING

INTRODUCTION

In January of 1970 students of the Perkins School of Theology in Dallas, Texas, met for an inter-term seminar on the Cultural Revolution and the Church. At the end of the course, prepared by the Ecumenical Institute in Chicago, they composed what can be considered a common creed. In that creed they wrote the following remarkable words:

> Standing before the mystery—man discovers that he has but one life to live—his own. To accept that fact, and to live it, is to receive grace and to discover that all of life is good. And when we die to our illusions that life is any other way than that, we discover the secret of all life: to die is to live. We are those who name this happening the Jesus Christ Event and reclaim for our time the message of the Biblical people—
> ("Bimonthly Newsletter" of The Ecumenical Institute, Vol. IV, No. 3, Jan.–Feb. 1970, p. 3.)

This powerful expression of faith makes it clear that the minister is the man who challenges us to *celebrate* life; that is, to turn away from fatalism and despair and to make our discovery that we have but one life to live into an ongoing recognition of God's work with man. But how can this celebration really be a human possibility? Our lives vibrate between two darknesses. We hesitantly come forth out of the darkness of birth and slowly vanish into the darkness of death. We move from dust to dust, from unknown to unknown, from mystery to mystery. We try to keep a vital balance on the thin rope that is stretched between two definitive endings we have never seen or understood. We are surrounded by the reality of the unseen, which fills every part of our life with a moment of terror but at the same time holds the secret mystery of our being alive.

The Christian minister is the one whose vocation is to make it possible for man not only to fully face his human situation but also to celebrate it in all its awesome reality.

But how do we celebrate life when we understand neither its ultimate terms nor the full meaning of what happens between them? Celebration seems the least appropriate response to our ambiguous condition. And if we want to celebrate, what kind of man can show us the way in which to realize our desires? These questions are essential to any attempt to discover the relationship between celebrating and spirituality. Therefore in this chapter I want to raise two questions: 1) how do we celebrate life? and 2) what kind of man is he who helps us to celebrate?

1. HOW DO WE CELEBRATE LIFE?

When we speak about celebration we tend rather easily to bring to mind happy, pleasant, gay festivities in which we can forget for a while the hardships of life and immerse ourselves in an atmosphere of music, dance, drinks, laughter, and a lot of cozy small-talk. But celebration in the Christian sense has very little to do with this. Celebration is only possible through the deep realization that life and death are never found completely separate. Celebration can only really come about where fear and love, joy and sorrow, tears and smiles can exist together. Celebration is the acceptance of life in a constantly increasing awareness of its preciousness. And life is precious not only because it can be seen, touched, and tasted, but also because it will be gone one day. When we celebrate a wedding, we celebrate a union as well as a departure, when we celebrate death we celebrate lost friendship as well as gained liberty. There can be tears after weddings and smiles after funerals. We can indeed make our sorrows, just as much as our joys, a part of our celebration of life in the deep realization that life and death are not opponents but do, in fact, kiss each other at every moment of our existence. When we are born we become free to breathe on our own but lose the safety of our mother's body; when we go to school we are free to join a greater society but lose a particular place in our family; when we marry we find a new partner but lose the special tie we had with our parents; when we find work we win our independence by making our own money but lose the stimulation of teachers and fellow students; when we receive children we discover a new world but lose much of our freedom to move; when we are promoted we become more important in the eyes of others but lose the chance to take many risks; when we retire we finally have the chance to do what we wanted but lose the support of being wanted. When we have been able to celebrate life in all these decisive moments where gaining and losing—that is, life and death—touched each other all the time, we will be able to celebrate even our own dying because we have learned from life that he who loses it can find it (cf. Mt. 16:25).

He who is able to celebrate life can prevent the temptation to search for clean joy or clean sorrow. Life is not wrapped in cellophane and protected against all infections. Celebration is the opposite of an escape from the realities of the full acceptance of life in its total complexity. If we now ask ourselves what the meaning of this acceptance is, we have to look at three main components of the act of accepting: affirming, remembering, and expecting.

1. Affirming

Celebrating is first of all the full affirmation of our present condition. We say with full consciousness: We are, we are here, we are now, and let it be that way. We can only really celebrate when we are present in the present. If anything has become clear, it is that we have to a large extent lost the capability to live in the present. Many so-called celebrations are not much more than a painful moment between bothersome preparations and boring after-talks. We can only celebrate if there *is* something present that can be celebrated. We cannot celebrate Christmas when there is nothing new born here and now, we cannot celebrate Easter when no new life becomes visible, we cannot celebrate Pentecost when there is no Spirit whatsoever to celebrate. Celebration is the recognition that something is there and needs to be made visible so that we can all say Yes to it.

I found a beautiful illustration of this in the meditation sessions of the members of the so-called *now generation*. Young people come together and for hours try to become present to each other and to recognize their togetherness as a precious reality. But how difficult this is! You can hardly take one step, one breath, without being flooded by thoughts and ideas that pull you away from yourself here and now and make you worry about thousands of little things. You find yourself thinking about your unfinished paper, your plans for tomorrow, or your last conversation. You find yourself asking thousands of unanswerable questions and looking at thousands of invisible pictures. You are not where you are but somewhere where you do not want to be. But when you become able, slowly and carefully, to push all these unwelcome intruders away from your mind you become aware that there has been something waiting for you of which you had not been aware, that you really can become present to your own self. At the same time you also become aware of the real presence of the other who is with you because, since he knows that his experience will find resonance in yours, he is willing to show you what he has discovered in his own presence.

In this context it becomes clear what praying together really means. It does not mean worrying together, but becoming present for each other in a very real way. Then it becomes possible to share ideas because they are really ours, to communicate feelings because they are actually there, to talk about concerns because they hurt us and we feel their pains in our own soul. Then the formulation of intentions is much more than an at-random choice from the many possible problems we can think of. It becomes, rather, an attempt to be visible and available to each other just as we are at this very moment. What we then ask from each other is not, first of all, to solve a problem or to give a hand, but to affirm each other in the many different ways we experience life. When this takes place, community starts to form and becomes a reality that can be celebrated as an affirmation of the multiformity of being in which we all take part.

2. Remembering

But nobody can really celebrate his life in the present when it is not meaningfully related to the past. The present cannot be experienced as present if the past cannot be remembered as past. A man without a past cannot celebrate the present and accept his life as his own.

Not too long ago I picked up a hitchhiker who told me that after a serious accident he had lost his memory of all the things that had happened to him during the last ten years. When he came back to the town where he lived, everything was new for him; no feelings, ideas, or associations were connected with the houses he saw and the streets he walked on. His friends had become strangers to him, and the things he had done had lost all their connections with his past. He had become a man without a history and, therefore, a man who could no longer give meaning to his present experience.

The way people relate to their own past is of crucial importance for their life experience. The past can become a prison in which you feel you are caught forever, or a constant reason to compliment yourself. Your past can make you deeply ashamed or guilt-ridden, but it can also be the cause of pride and self-content. Some people will say with remorse: "If I could live my life again, I certainly would do it differently"; others will say with self-assertion: "You might think I am an old, weak man, but look at those trophies there; I won those when I was young." Memory is one of the greatest sources of human happiness and human suffering. If we want to celebrate our lives in the present, we cannot cut off ourselves from our past. We are instead, invited to look at our history as the sequence of events that brought us where we are now and that help us to understand what it means to be here at this moment in this world.

He who celebrates life will not make his past a prison nor a source of pride, but will face the facts of history and fully accept them as the elements that allow him to claim his experience as his own.

When we commemorate during a liturgical celebration those who have gone before us, we do much more than direct a pious thought to our deceased family and friends; we recognize that we stand in the midst of history and that the affirmation of our present condition is grounded in the recognition that we were brought to where we are now by the innumerable people who lived *their* lives before we were given the chance to live *ours*.

3. *Expecting*

But besides affirming life and remembering it, celebration is filled with expectations for the future. If the past had the last word, a man would imprison himself more and more the older he became. If the present were the ultimate moment of satisfaction, man would cling to it with a hedonistic eagerness, trying to squeeze the last drop of life out of it. But the present holds promises and reaches out to the horizons of life, and this makes it possible for us to embrace our future as well as our past in the moment of celebration.

The truth of this was brought home very forcefully to me by a recent painful experience. In January of last year a friend of mine died in Tunisia, where he had gone to work for a few months to help the people who suffered from a terrible flood. His parents, simple farmers living in a small village, expected much from their son, who had been the first university student in the family. His death in a distant country unknown to most of the people of the village paralyzed his family and friends and came as a shock to the entire town.

The most horrible week was the week when there was
nothing but the telegram, that ridiculous piece of paper
saying what could not be believed. But when the body
was flown back and brought into the village, the death of
this student could be celebrated. The fact that he died
while really doing good could be affirmed, and his past
could be remembered as a chain of events that had led to
the tragic accident. But I am deeply convinced that it became a real celebration only because of the fact that new
life became visible around the body of this young man.
Suddenly people realized what it meant to give one's life for
others; men and women who never had heard about Tunisia
started to talk about it and to ask what kind of men those
strange-looking Mohammedans really were. People from the
city met people from the village and became friends. And
after the body was covered with sand people began to be
aware that their world had become wider, their ideas larger,
and their perspectives deeper. The present indeed held promises for the future. This became clear when a few months
later many more students made plans to continue what their
friend had begun.

So celebrating means the affirmation of the present, which
becomes fully possible only by remembering the past and
expecting more to come in the future. But celebrating in
this sense very seldom takes place. Nothing is as difficult
as really accepting one's own life. More often than not the
present is denied, the past becomes a source of complaints,
and the future is looked upon as a reason for despair or
apathy.

When Jesus came to redeem mankind, He came to free us
from the boundaries of time. Through Him it became clear
not only that God is with us wherever our presence is in

time or space, but also that our past does not have to be forgotten or denied but can be remembered and forgiven, and that we are still waiting for Him to come back and reveal to us what remains unseen. When Jesus left his Apostles He gave them bread and wine in memory of what He did so that He could stay in their presence until the moment of His return. The word Eucharist, which means thanksgiving, expresses a way of accepting life in which the past and the future are brought together in the present moment. This thanksgiving is meant to be a way of living that makes it possible to really celebrate life. Frequently, this Eucharistic celebration of life takes place elsewhere than where it is formally planned. Life is not always really celebrated where liturgies are held. Sometimes it is, but quite often it is not. Perhaps we have to become more sensitive to people and places where no one ever talks about liturgical reform or changes, but where life is fully affirmed in the deepest Eucharistic sense.

II. WHAT KIND OF MAN IS HE WHO MAKES CELEBRATION POSSIBLE?

When we now wish to speak about the minister who enables man to celebrate, we are faced with the fact that for a man in our culture celebrating has become an extremely difficult thing to do. It seems that the Christian invitation to celebrate, to accept your life as the only life you have, to live it and accept it as good, has perhaps become the most difficult challenge modern man is facing.

We live in a culture in which the words of Jesus: "Do not worry about tomorrow, tomorrow will take care of itself" (Mt. 6:34), sound beautiful and romantic, but completely unrealistic. We live in such a utilitarian society

that even our most intimate moments have become subject
to the question: "What is the purpose of it?"

Modern man does not just eat and drink but has business
lunches and fund-raising dinners. He does not just go horseback riding or swimming—he also invites his companions to
do a little business on horseback or even in the pool. He
does not just exercise his body or listen to beautiful songs,
but he also has become involved in a tremendous industry
of sports and music. And he always keeps on believing
that the real thing is going to happen tomorrow. In this
kind of life the past has degenerated into a series of used
or misused opportunities, the present into a constant concern about accomplishments, and the future into a make-
believe paradise where man hopes to finally receive what he
always wanted but the existence of which he basically doubts.

A life like this cannot be celebrated because we are constantly concerned with changing it into something else,
always trying to do something to it, get something out of it,
and make it fit our many plans and projects. We go to
meetings, conferences, and congresses. We critically evaluate
our part, discuss how to do it better in the future, and
worry whether or not our great design will ever work out.

Our culture is a working, hurrying, and worrying culture
with many opportunities except the opportunity to celebrate
life.

Insofar as this is true, we wonder how Christian our
culture really is. It is a remarkable fact that the first and
strongest reactions against this style of life have not come
from the churches but from the many people living on
the fringes of our society trying to give shape to what
Theodore Roszak has called "the counter-culture." It is in

the youthful opposition against our technocratic society that we truly find some authentic elements of a celebrating style of life. In the voices of those who announce the new counter-culture we might hear sounds familiar to the Christian ear.

Roszak writes:

> The primary project of our counter-culture is: to proclaim a new heaven and a new earth, so vast, so marvelous, that the inordinate claims of technical expertise must of necessity withdraw in the presence of such splendor to a subordinate and marginal status in the lives of man—we must be prepared to consider the scandalous possibility that wherever the visionary imagination grows bright, magic, that old antagonist of science, renews itself, transmitting our workday reality into something bigger, perhaps more frightening, certainly more adventurous than the lesser rationality of objective conscience can ever countenance.
>
> (*The Making of a Counter-Culture*, Anchor Books, Doubleday, New York, 1969, p. 240.)

This is announcing a new life that can be celebrated. But where does this leave ministers and priests who, though still having many faithful people in their churches, nonetheless do not find members of the counter-culture in their audiences? As long as the minister does no more than use Sunday to soften the pains of the week, his teaching, preaching, counseling, and organizing remain services to a life that cannot be celebrated.

But if he wants to show the way to celebration, he has to be a special kind of man. He has to be and become more and more an obedient man—that is, a man who allows himself to be guided by the voices he hears. He has to be obedient to the voices of nature, to the voices of people, and to the voice of God.

Let us therefore look at the spirituality of the celebrant in the perspective of obedience.

1. *Obedience to the voice of nature*

He who wants to help others to celebrate, first of all has to be obedient to the voices of nature and able to translate their message for his fellow man. Perhaps we have a lot to learn from the Indians here. It seems that we have become so concerned with mastering nature that we have become deaf to the voices of the rivers, the trees, the birds, and the flowers which are constantly telling us about our own condition of life, our beauty, and our mortality.

A Wintu Indian says:

> The white people never cared for land or deer or bear. When we Indians kill meat, we eat it all up. When we dig roots, we make little holes . . . We shake down acorns and pine nuts. We don't chop down trees. We only use dead wood. But the white people plow up the ground, pull up the trees, kill everything. The tree says, "Don't, I am sore. Don't hurt me." But they chop it down and cut it up. The spirit of the land hates them . . . The Indians never hurt anything, but the white people destroy all.
>
> (op. cit., p. 245.)

The Indian knows he has to become more and more a part of nature, a brother of all creatures, so that he can find his real place in this world. He makes his artwork in obedience to nature. In his masks human and animal faces merge, in his pottery he uses vegetables, such as the gourd, for models. It is nature that teaches him the forms he can make with his own hands.

It is not so difficult to understand why, through all the ages, people searching for the meaning of life tried to live as close to nature as possible. Not only St. Benedict, St. Francis, and St. Bruno in the olden days, but also Thomas Merton, who lived in the woods of Kentucky, and the Benedictine monks, who built their monastery in an isolated canyon in New Mexico. It is not so strange that many young people are leaving the cities and going out into the country to find peace by listening to the voices of nature. And nature indeed speaks: the birds to St. Francis, the trees to the Indians, the river to Siddhartha. And the closer we come to nature, the closer we touch the core of life when we celebrate. Nature makes us aware of the preciousness of life. Nature tells us that life is precious not only because it is, but also because it does not have to be.

I remember sitting day after day at the same table in a dull restaurant where I had to eat my lunch. There was a beautiful red rose in a small vase in the middle of the table. I looked at the rose with sympathy and enjoyed its beauty. Every day I talked with my rose. But then I became suspicious. Because while my mood was changing during the week from happy to sad, from disappointed to angry, from energetic to apathetic, my rose was always the same. And moved by my suspicion I lifted my fingers to the rose and touched it. It was a plastic thing. I was deeply offended and never went back there to eat.

We cannot talk with plastic nature because it cannot tell us the real story about life and death. But if we are sensitive to the voice of nature, we might be able to hear sounds from a world where man and nature both find their shape. We will never fully understand the meaning of the sacramental signs of bread and wine when they do not make us realize that the whole of nature is a sacrament pointing to a reality far beyond itself. The presence of Christ in the Eucharist becomes a "special problem" only when we have lost our sense of His presence in all that is, grows, lives, and dies. What happens during a Sunday celebration can only be a real celebration when it reminds us in the fullest sense of what continually happens every day in the world which surrounds us. Bread is more than bread; wine is more than wine: it is God with us—not as an isolated event once a week but as the concentration of a mystery about which all of nature speaks day and night.

Therefore, wasting food is not just a sin because there are still so many hungry people in this world. It is a sin because it is an offense against the sacramental reality of all we eat and drink. But if we become more and more aware of the voices of all that surrounds us and grow in respect and reverence for nature, then we also will be able to truly care for man who is embedded in nature like a sapphire in a golden ring.

2. *Obedience to people*

For the man who wants to bring others to the celebration of their lives, however, obedience to people is even more important than obedience to nature. A man who is really able to listen to people will be able to recognize their desire as well as their fear of celebrating. Celebration asks for the willingness to be enraptured by the greatness of the mystery which surrounds man, and for many, who would like to be in real touch with the ground of their own existence, there is a deep-seated anxiety about being absorbed by it and losing their identity. Man cannot live without the sun, but he knows that by coming too close to it he will be burned. The utilitarian man has built a thick wall between himself and the source of his existence out of fear of total absorption. But that same wall dooms him to live a cold and alienated life. He knows this and desperately asks the minister, who should know how to be close without being absorbed, to offer a way to participate in what is real life.

Roszak expresses this deep human desire when he writes:

> It is, at last, reality itself that must be participated in, must be seen, touched, breathed with the conviction that here is the ultimate ground of our existence, available to all, capable of ennobling by its majesty the life of every man who opens himself. It is participation of this order —experiential and not merely political—that alone can guarantee the dignity and autonomy of the individual citizen. The strange youngsters who don cowbells and primitive talismans and who take to the public parks or wilderness to improvise outlandish communal ceremonies are in reality seeking to ground democracy safely beyond the culture of expertise.
>
> (op. cit., p. 265.)

But what many young people do is, in fact, part of the desire of every man: to live life to the fullest, on the deepest possible level. The minister or priest is challenged to offer the way. He is looked upon as a man who has closer contact with this reality than many others, not as a personal privilege but as a peculiar gift which he is to share with others. When Roszak describes the shaman, he describes at the same time the service every minister and priest should offer: to be like an "artist, who lays his work before the community in the hope that through it, as through a window, the reality he has fathomed can be witnessed by all who give attention" (op. cit., p. 260).

By participating in ritual, the community is able to see, feel, touch, and fully experience without fear of absorption the reality that the minister has discovered for them. In Roszak's words: "Ritual is the [minister's] way of broadcasting his vision, it is his instructive offering. If the [minister's] work is successful, the community's sense of reality will become expansive" (*op. cit.*, p. 260). The great temptation is to consider the priest's or minister's closeness to the mystery of God as a privilege instead of a responsibility, and to turn his own vocation into a special status and his ministry into an exploitive enterprise. But when he really can be obedient to his people he will recognize their deep desire to see what he saw, to hear what he heard, to touch what he touched, and to break down the wall that separates them from the "Unseen" (W. James) Reality of the universe. Then he will keep searching for ways and channels, forms and rituals, songs, dances, and gestures that enable man to come into vibrant contact with the Holy without fear. Then he will make it possible for his fellow man to take down his scaffolding and to freely celebrate life.

3. *Obedience to God*

But does the priest and the minister have any peculiar gift which he can share? Does he have a vision he can offer to help others see? Is he any closer than anyone else to the source of his existence, and does he know, feel, and see more deeply the condition in which man is imprisoned but from which he wants to become free?

If the answer is *No*, we may rightly wonder if he will ever be able to help man celebrate life. He who is set apart to lead people to the heart of God's mystery will never be able to do so when he is blind, does not know the way, or is afraid to approach the throne of God.

Ordination means the recognition and affirmation of the fact that a man has gone beyond the walls of fear, lives in

intimate contact with the God of the living, and has a
burning desire to show others the way to Him. Ordination
does not make anybody anything but is the solemn recognition of the fact that this man has been able to be obedient
to God, to hear His voice and understand His call, and that
he can offer others the way to that same experience. Therefore, the minister who wants to make celebration possible
is a man of prayer. Only a man of prayer can lead others
to celebration because everyone who comes in contact with
him realizes that he draws his powers from a source they
cannot easily locate but they know is strong and deep.
The freedom that gives him a certain independence is not
authoritarian or distant. Rather, it makes him rise above
the immediate needs and most urgent desires of the people
around him. He is deeply moved by things happening around
him, but he does not allow himself to be crushed by them.
He listens attentively, speaks with a self-evident authority,
but does not easily get excited or nervous. In all he says or
does, he proves to have a vision that guides his life. To
that vision he is obedient. It makes him distinguish sharply
between what is important and what is not. He is not insensi-
tive to what excites people, but he evaluates their needs
differently by seeing them in the perspective of his vision.
He is happy and content when people listen to him,
but he does not want to form cliques. He does not attach
himself to anybody exclusively. What he says sounds convincing and obvious, but he does not force his opinion on
anybody and is not irritated when people do not accept
his ideas or do not fulfill his will. All this shows that his
vision is what counts for him and that he strives to make it
come true.

But he also has an inner freedom in respect to this ideal.
He knows he will not see his purpose realized, and he
considers himself only as a guide to it. He is impressively

free toward his own life. From his actions it becomes clear that he considers his own existence of secondary importance. He does not live to keep himself alive but to build a new world of which he has already seen the first images and which so appeals to him that the borderline between his life and his death loses its definitiveness. This is a man who not only celebrates life but can also make others desire to do the same.

And so we have seen how obedience to nature, to people, and to God are three characteristics of the man who wants to be a servant in the celebration of life. No man can claim for himself to be such a celebrant. Only Jesus could because only He was obedient to God and creation unto death, even death on the Cross. It is on the Cross that He became the celebrant of life in the full sense because it was there that death was conquered and life regained in the total act of obedience. In this way, anyone who calls himself a minister can only consider himself a weak reflection of He who gave His life on the Cross and made it available to all who are called to celebrate their lives as children of the same Father.

CONCLUSION

The main idea of this chapter is that obedience to God and creation is the basic condition for being a celebrant of life. If a minister claims to be a man who wants others to fully accept their lives as their own by affirmation, remembrance, and expectation, he himself is challenged to be a servant of life who can listen to the voices of nature, people, and God and announce what he has heard to those who want to join him in the act of celebration.

Through celebration we enter into the Kingdom of Heaven. But Jesus said: "Unless you change and become like little children you will never enter the Kingdom of Heaven" (Mt. 18:3). It is through childlike obedience that life becomes a way to the Kingdom. And if you have ever offered bread and wine to God on the rim of the Grand Canyon, you might have then experienced that we can really celebrate when humility has made us free. We are only a very small part of history and have only one short life to live, but when we take the fruits of our labor in our hands and stretch our arms to God in the deep belief that He hears us and accepts our gifts, then we know that all of our life is given, given to celebrate.

CONCLUSION

If there is any sentence in the Gospel that expresses in a very concentrated way everything I have tried to say in the five chapters of this book, it is the sentence spoken by Jesus to his Apostles the day before His death: "A man can have no greater love than to lay down his life for his friends" (John 15:13).

For me these words summarize the meaning of all Christian ministry. If teaching, preaching, individual pastoral care, organizing, and celebrating are acts of service that go beyond the level of professional expertise, it is precisely because in these acts the minister is asked to lay down his own life for his friends. There are many people who, through long training, have reached a high level of competence in terms of the understanding of human behavior, but few who are willing to lay down their own lives for others and make their weakness a source of creativity. For many individuals professional training means power. But the minister, who takes off his clothes to wash the feet of his friends, is powerless, and his training and formation are meant to enable him to face his own weakness without fear and make it available to others. It is exactly this creative weakness that gives the ministry its momentum.

Teaching becomes ministry when the teacher moves beyond the transference of knowledge and is willing to offer his own life experience to his student so that paralyzing anxiety can be removed, new liberating insight can come about, and real learning can take place. Preaching becomes ministry when the preacher moves beyond the "telling of the story" and makes his own deepest self available to his hearers so that they will be able to receive the Word of God. Individual care becomes ministry when he who wants to be of help moves beyond the careful balance of give and take with a willingness to risk his own life and remain faithful to his suffering fellow man even when his own name and fame is in danger. Organizing becomes ministry when the organizer moves beyond his desire for concrete results and looks at his world with the unwavering hope for a total renewal. Celebrating becomes ministry when the celebrant moves beyond the limits of protective rituals to an obedient acceptance of life as a gift.

Although none of these tasks of service can ever be fulfilled without careful preparation and proved competence, none can ever be called ministry when this competence is not grounded in the radical commitment to lay down one's own life in the service of others. Ministry means the ongoing attempt to put one's own search for God, with all the moments of pain and joy, despair and hope, at the disposal of those who want to join this search but do not know how. Therefore, ministry in no way is a privilege. Instead, it is the core of the Christian life. No Christian is a Christian without being a minister. There are many more forms of ministry than the five I have discussed in this book, which usually fill the daily life of the ordained minister and priest. But whatever form the Christian ministry takes, the basis is always the same: to lay down one's life for one's friends.

But why does a man lay down his life for his friends? There is only one answer to that question: to give new life. All functions of the ministry are life giving. Whether a man teaches, preaches, counsels, plans, or celebrates, his aim is to open new perspectives, to offer new insight, to give new strength, to break through the chains of death and destruction, and to create new life which can be affirmed. In short—to make his weakness creative.

So, if a man wants to be a minister, let him be happy to make his weaknesses his special boast so that the power of Christ may stay over him . . . for when he is weak then he is strong (cf. St. Paul, 2 Cor. 12:9–10).

But although no man can live and keep living without need for this ministry, it seems that for many people, who are exposed to the growing destructive potentials of our world and have seen the most ruthless and cruel annihilation of life during their own short history, Christianity does not seem able to offer this indispensable ministry. When they hear about the life of Jesus and His Apostles, they wonder what that story has to do with this age of atomic power. When they are told that their lives play a meaningful role in the great history of mankind, in which the redemption through the death of Christ has to become more and more visible, they, in fact, do not see much more than an increasing escalation of war, poverty, cruelty, and senseless destruction of their environment. When they are comforted with the idea that this life is not final and that they will find its continuation in a world after this, their question is whether there is much here that calls for continuation and whether it makes sense to think about some new life in a vague future when even words like "tomorrow," "next week," "next year," and "later" are losing their meaning in a world that can kill not only man but also his history.

Perhaps the apparent crisis in the Christian ministry is directly related to the fact that modern man, exposed to so many fearful and widely contrasting experiences and ideas, has hardly any meaningful roots in his past nor much expectation for the future. Robert Jay Lifton speaks of a "world-wide sense of . . . historical dislocation," which he describes as "a break in the sense of connection which men have long felt with the vital and nourishing symbols of their cultural tradition—symbols revolving around family, idea systems, religion, and the life cycle in general." ("Protean Man," *Partisan Review*, 1968, p. 16.)

But if our atomic age—which is able to destroy not just individuals and families but whole cultures and their histories, whole countries and their chances for rebirth—has caused many people to lose confidence in the Christian ministry, the question is whether we have fully understood what it means today to lay down one's life for one's friends.

Maybe we have to look beyond the institutional church to grasp the full implications of this call, because words such as concentration, meditation, and contemplation are again used today with great reverence by thousands of young people who will never think of going to a church or consulting a Christian minister. In a great variety of ways they try to break through their confusion and restlessness to find in the center of their own experience something that can make them reach beyond their own limited consciousness. They are experimenting with new methods of relating to each other, new ways of non-violent communication, new approaches to the experience of oneness and union, new means of mutual care, and new attempts to celebrate their lives. They borrow symbols not only from Christian tradition but also from Buddhism and Hinduism; they try to broaden their sensitivities by natural and artificial stimuli such as flowers, incense, and hallucinogenic drugs. They form communities, share their possessions, and read, sing, and prophesy to experience a new sense of freedom.

It is no exaggeration to say that, while the churches become emptier year after year, new forms of ministry are being sought on the periphery of Christianity and that teaching, preaching, caring, planning, and celebrating are appearing in new ways in the many catacombs of our modern cities. In the middle of our chaotic world we have become increasingly aware of the permanent threat of total destruction and cry desperately for a new "spirituality" that enables men to come to terms with their search for meaning. This new spirituality is described by Lifton as "the path of experiential transcendence—of seeking a sense of immortality in the way the mystics always have, through psychic experience of such great intensity that time and death are, in effect, eliminated" (op. cit., p. 27).

It is painful to realize that very few ministers are able to offer the rich mystical tradition of Christianity as a source of rebirth for the generation searching for new life in the midst of the debris of a faltering civilization. Perhaps our self-consciousness, fear of rejection, and preoccupation with church quarrels prevent us from being free to experience the transcendent Spirit of God, which can renew our hearts and our world as well. Perhaps we are not ready yet to give the so-much-needed guidance to the thousands who engage themselves in a risky experimentation with the powers of the unseen. Perhaps we ourselves have lost contact with these powers and can only qualify the stories of the catacombs as weird, dangerous, and signs of immaturity. But I am afraid that the many obvious mistakes, failures, and unintelligible experiments blind us to the fact that underneath all of this there is a deep desire for new insight, new understanding, and most of all, new life.

If I can trust my own feelings and limited experiences with young students, it seems that we are approaching a period of an increased search for spirituality that is the experience of God in this very moment of our existence. When there is so little in the past to hold on to and so little in the future to look forward to, the reality that can give meaning to one's life must be experienced here and now.

A twenty-year-old Catholic student, who considered his church completely irrelevant for his needs but who was desperately searching for meaning in his life, said to me: "We tried drugs and it did not work; we tried sex and it did not work; the next thing will be suicide—in the coming years you will see the number of suicides sky-rocketing." The only possible response to this seems to be to rediscover the transcending power of the spiritual life by which man is able to stand strong even when surrounded by shifting ideologies, crumbling political, social, and religious structures, and a constant threat of war and total destruction. It may be extremely difficult for modern man to feel close to Jesus of Nazareth as a man who lived in another world; it may be even more difficult to look forward to the day of His return; but more than ever it may be possible to experience the Spirit of Christ as a living Spirit who makes it possible to break through the boundaries of our imprisoned existence and makes us free to work for a new world.

But this way of the transcendental experience is a way that requires ministry. It calls for men and women who do not shy away from careful preparation, solid formation, and qualified training but at the same time are free enough to break through the restrictive boundaries of disciplines and specialties in the conviction that the Spirit moves beyond professional expertise. It calls for Christians who are willing to develop their sensitivity to God's presence in their own lives, as well as in the lives of others, and to offer their experiences as a way of recognition and liberation to their fellow men. It calls for ministers in the true sense, who lay down their own lives for their friends, helping them to distinguish between the constructive and the destructive spirits and making them free for the discovery of God's life-giving Spirit in the midst of this maddening world. It calls for creative weakness.

EPILOGUE

When I look back at the way I wrote this book, I begin to realize that it is a very personal book. In fact, it is an attempt to articulate ideas and feelings about the ministry based on the ups and downs of my own experiences. I hoped that a careful reflection on these experiences could throw some light on the different questions I had asked myself and give some insight into the direction I want to go from here.

I also hoped that my "confession" could be of some help to others in the ongoing discussion about the value and meaning of the Christian ministry. Therefore, the conclusion of this book does not want to suggest the end of a discussion but the beginning of one. In fact, this discussion has already become part of this book, because while presenting the different chapters to priests and ministers, to sisters and social workers, to parents and students, I became more and more aware that many people had completely different experiences from those I had and could hardly recognize themselves in the ideas I tried to formulate. When I was confronted with so many questions and criticisms my first inclination was to go back to the text and start all over again. But then I realized that this was impossible, because I could not change my own past and had to accept the limitation attached to being personal. My friend Don McNeill even made me see that it would be much more realistic and in line with my own conviction if I presented the questions and criticisms at the end of this book instead of smuggling the untested answers into the text itself.

Well, there are many unanswered questions. And every chapter has its own. I should like to formulate some of them here.

On teaching:

> What you say about the relationship between student and teacher may be interesting for a college situation, but what about grade school and high school? Does your whole idea not become very romantic when you are confronted with the task of teaching mathematics to small children who can hardly sit quiet for a minute?

On preaching:

> Don't you have to be a trained psychologist to be available to others in the way you suggest. What about the ordinary priest who has to get up into that pulpit every week? Aren't you a little too demanding? And, after all, is the direct presentation of the Word of God, welcome or unwelcome, not more important than the subtle clarification of people's feelings?

On individual pastoral care:

> I work as a chaplain in a prison with twenty men in one cell. When I come in the cell the prisoners fight for the chance to talk with me and to ask me for very concrete help—to find out where their children are, to visit their wives, to ask when their trial will be, to find some

medicine, etc., etc. What does it mean to be a pastor for these men? It seems I do not have to go beyond professionalism to fulfill the task of four different professions at once!

On organizing:

If you had been a priest in the ghettos you never would have said what you did. You missed the point completely. You are simply soft peddling the whole issue. You suggest an unrealistic detachment in an emergency situation.

On celebrating:

What about the children who never have lived in nature and probably never will. What about the millions of men living in the ever-growing cities? How should they celebrate?

I do not know the answers to these questions and criticisms. They are undoubtedly a convincing illustration of the limitations of my own ideas. But I hope that they also show the value and necessity of the sharing of experiences as a primary condition for an ongoing search for a spirituality of ministry.